Good Times in Dystopia

Good Times in Dystopia

George F.

zero books

Winchester, UK
Washington, USA

JOHN HUNT PUBLISHING

First published by Zero Books, 2019
Zero Books is an imprint of John Hunt Publishing Ltd., No. 3 East St., Alresford,
Hampshire SO24 9EE, UK
office@jhpbooks.com
www.johnhuntpublishing.com
www.zero-books.net

For distributor details and how to order please visit the 'Ordering' section on our website.

ISBN: 978 1 78904 190 3
978 1 78904 191 0 (ebook)
Library of Congress Control Number: 2018953743

A CIP catalogue record for this book is available from the British Library.

Design: Stuart Davies

UK: Printed and bound by CPI Group (UK) Ltd, Croydon, CR0 4YY
US: Printed and bound by Thomson-Shore, 7300 West Joy Road, Dexter, MI 48130

Contents

Everything in this book actually happened,
mostly, although a certain licence has been taken with names,
places and people to protect the innocent and the guilty.
It is meant to be read as a piece of creative non-fiction.

For Mierda & Sheize

good time
[gud-taim]

[noun]

1. the right moment to do something or for something to happen.

2. in legal terms, time deducted from an inmate's sentence for good behaviour while in prison.

dystopia
[dis-toh-pee-uh]

[noun]

1. from the Greek δυσ- and τόπος,(alternatively, **cacotopia**, **kakotopia**, or simply **anti-utopia**) is a community or society that is undesirable or frightening. It is translated as "not-good place", an antonym of utopia.

2. a society characterised by human misery, as squalor, oppression, disease and overcrowding.

Bad times, hard times, this is what people keep saying; but let us live well, and times shall be good. We are the times: Such as we are, such are the times.
St Augustine of Hippo

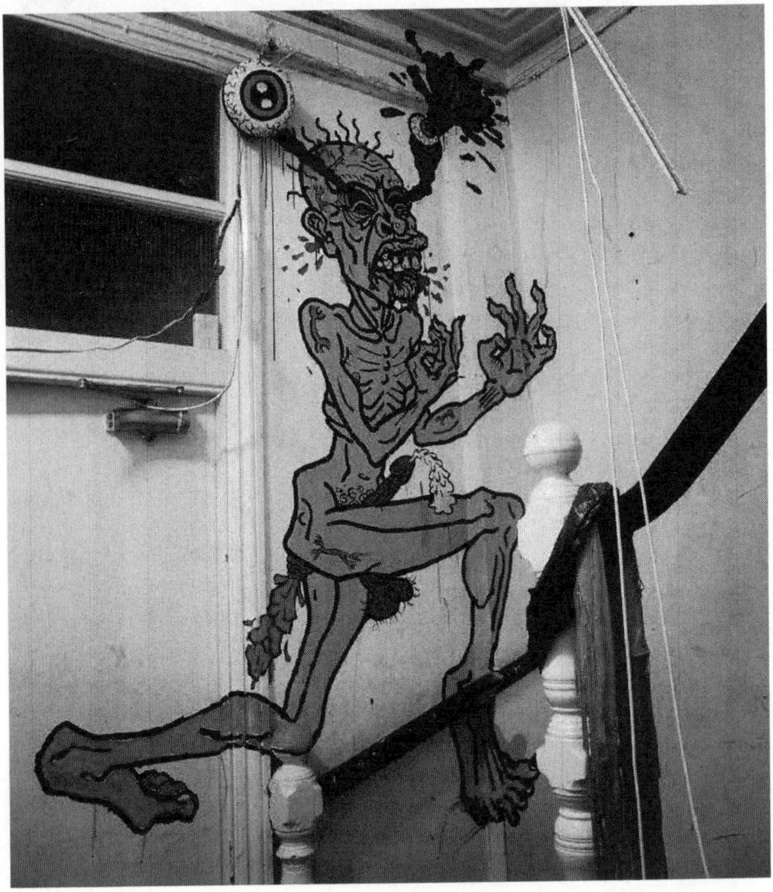

1

Shoreditch, Sometime in July

The moon hung over the planet Earth, a dead thing over a dying thing.
John Fowles

The toilet is vomiting black shit. Toxic, vile, noxious – the rejected bile of the City of London spuming back up from the gullet under the street. Three maniacs in white overalls are jigging around, ankle deep in filth, their hair a red, black and green tricolour fire flashing against shitsmears and white suits. I bring them four cans of beer, and they flick the crud off from their gloved hands to clutch and crack them, laughing amidst choking fumes like sewage tear gas. The beer foams, clean and snowy, in contrast to the bubbling bilious blackness of the bog blowing black bubbles in the back of the Shitness School. It won't stop. We won't stop. So we grab the jigsaw and cut a perfect golden triangle into the floor to let the coal black frackshite drain into the empty office space below.

Once that gaping floor-anus is opened, I cannot resist it. I'll shit directly into the space ten metres below to avoid crapping in an empty pizza box and being caught on the stairs delivering it to the street.

"What's in there?"

"You don't want to know."

Once on the street I'll be sure to bury the forbidden crap-package at the bottom of the trash pile to prevent some unfortunate street-skipper excitedly scooping a box of hot poop off the floor to open it to nothing but disappointment. I try not to inflict my shit on other people.

It's raining down one side of the room I am sharing. The

damp creeps across the carpet tiles inexorably towards the sofa cushions I've shoved against one wall. The sound of running water pouring down the walls into the rooms below seems a mocking irony to the fact we have no toilet and shower. I can wash – awkwardly – with a kettle and running water in the dilapidated kitchen, but most of the time I wonder why to bother.

Sunrise on the suicide-shelf at the top of the building where I stood on my birthday and considered that drop into the street below as a gateway to something other than the misery and torment that I had sunk into. Sunrise each time when we brought the randoms and the strangers and the passers-by up on to the heights on the edge of the city and tried our utmost to open them up and fuck them. In the end, it would all unravel around us and there would be nothing left but everything else. I wept there and considered the abyss but in the end I was not as strong as others around – or perhaps I was too weak. Eternity's fucking sunrise – dangled upon the edge with a beer in hand and not sure whether to cry or to laugh or to puke or to whip my fucking cock out.

At night, we crouch in the window-sill shrieking drunken madness at the passers-by of Shoreditch High Street, beckoning them in to join us beneath the gigantic twisted mural of an emaciated Auschwitz survivor, his eyes exploding from their sockets, painted over the alarm bell that signals each guest that arrives at the door, simultaneously evacuating his bowels and ejaculating in an ecstatic death-throw down one wall.

Mierda painted it, and I like an apostatic apprentice bounded around her scrawling dubious ditties and sloganeering over the walls behind her, happy and in glee to be free and creating amidst the shite and detritus of the city.

The rats run rabid – scurrying and seeking and clawing around us with their little human hands. The wolf stalks – barking a savage sonata to each guest that enters – a challenge and a question and a summons. When I first meet her, the wolf terrifies me into paralysis. I stand and watch frozen and impotent, awaiting the next move – until I realise that the thunder and fury was just that – noise echoing around the clouds and concretising something that would be otherwise abstract and intangible. All the noise, all the mania, all the terror – something real and unreal at the same moment. The echo of a shout into a cave. A cave set in the cliffs mounting the rivers of traffic and hubbub that flow through the City and out into the East End. All our noise and chaos is a hollow echo and tribute to the nightmarish babel that slurries past us every weekend on the streets.

We skip people like we might skip food – fishing them out of the bins to gorge ourselves upon them. Yet when I manage it, I am horrified at the callousness of the exchange. One I manage to fish comes back, exclaims at the rooftop delights of the city looming iridescent and sparkling above us, retires to my shared room half-soggy with rain, then fled to a taxi without so much as an exchange of numbers. When I encounter her again on Great Eastern Street a week later, spotty and empussed, she blithers empty excuses and averts her eyes. I had been fucked and chucked and had no further care for the experience. I'd fucked her like she asked, lying down on top of her beneath a canopy of electric stars, unfettered by her proclamation that she was on her period, exerting to ejaculation despite my broken ribs and crippling liver pain. Afterwards, she'd sucked in futility upon my flaccid cock, hungrily trying to coax it back into action, her sexuality suddenly vampiric, I'd been snared by a Shoreditch succubus.

And so what if I was nothing but food for others? Hadn't I returned excited and elated with bottles of shoplifted beer to find my lover in bed with another? What did any animal acts such as fucking mean between strangers? I was no better and the ones I desired no worse. We were now but meat-puppets jigging on the strings of our desires...

yet still I was surprised.. –

– the Mierda found a way into me.

2

Down With The Shitness

We are close to dead. There are faces and bodies like gorged maggots on the dance floor, on the highway, in the city, in the stadium; they are a host of chemical machines who swallow the product of chemical factories, aspirin, preservatives, stimulant, relaxant, and breathe out their chemical wastes into a polluted air. The sense of a long last night over civilization is back again.
Norman Mailer

Some days, all I can do is lie in bed and stare at the ceiling, pretending that I am dead.

The ceiling is warped, corners blackening with mould, and rainwater pours down one half of the far wall. But I do not mind, because I am dead.

I guess I have been dead since I stood on the edge of the roof and looked down at Shoreditch's gum-spattered pavements. Maybe I died before and didn't realise, but that moment was a clear threshold where I made the choice to die.

I didn't die physically, but something died inside, and although I stepped back from the edge to see what else might happen, I became a ghost, haunting the remnants of this destroyed and defiled metropolis, barely visible, living in the cracks and shadows of the City of London. I become a wraith of petrol fumes evaporating in the bright summer sunshine – people in floppy hats and vintage printed shirts with Ray-Bans bump into me on Brick Lane, their noses wrinkling at the acrid stench – but in the greying summer drizzle of acid rain I attain at least solidity enough for the water to smack off my ragged *jaegarjacken*.

It's not so bad being dead, especially in the bed. I lie here for hours, days even, feeling hollow and expired. I emerge and head downstairs to the front room, and the banging and screaming and mania doesn't bother me so much. Piles of trash and tools and rotting food fill the carpeted walls, and it is not so bad. I join in with the other Hungry Ghosts – screaming and drinking and falling over – and death doesn't seem so dreary. Most of all, I enjoy the miserable peace of my soggy mattress in my dripping room, a watery purgatory lost somewhere beneath a collapsing roof.

At times, I take my dead self back up to the roof, and stare wistfully out over Shoreditch's Babylonian vistas: at teams of visceral drinkers squashed into the simmering neon of the Drunken Monkey, at the steady rumble of traffic up Great Eastern Street, at the milky mural painted on the railway bridge that reads *"We Have To Adore and Endure Each Other"*, at the distant squat bulk of the Chariot's sauna behind the wine supermarket. All the fashionable ant people parading up and down, far below us, and over it all, just off to the west, the silvery, glittering towers of the city, watching over us all like the tumescent phalluses of huge metallic sentinels.

Dead – I feel very little but the wind blowing through me, occasional patches of sun warming my dead bones, or the passing rain wetting my face. I wonder what dead people do.

For one, they write. Nostalgia and reminiscence come very easily to the dead.

They drink. It helps the dead to forget, to numb the pain.

They talk to the living, who surprisingly seem to hear it, or at least make requisite and appropriate responses. I wonder if everyone else around me is actually dead as well. Maybe they don't realise it.

The dead steal from shops. When you're dead, you don't worry so much about the consequences of shoplifting. As a dead ghost, I attract a remarkably slight amount of attention taking bottles of beer, wine – red and ginger – from the shelves and unceremoniously shoving them into my trousers. Security guards sometimes apprehend me at the doors, and an unpleasant scene ensues, with unemployed actors playing hired guards arguing with a dead person about what is in his pocket. Once on Great Eastern Street I breeze in like a poltergeist, take hold of a crate of beer and flee, running down the street to the Shitness School and safety.

Occasionally the dead must eat.

Awi, Grizzly and Mierda come back with a mega-skip: a whole trolley overloaded with cider, weak lagers, fruit juices, blackcurrants, bananas, bags of crisps, grapes, chocolate, all the gak. We load it up dutifully in the corner of the front room and proceed to slowly and steadily work our way through it. Naiad joins us, and Awi suggests we watch a movie together, projected on the wall.

It takes a while for him to sort out the technical details, but eventually the four of us sprawl on mattresses, drinking watery lager and eating crisps, and watch a documentary about a man several of us know from another squat. A methamphetamine cook. There is a documentary about his life in the Czech Republic, where he used to live with his wife and children, sometime in a dreamlike past.

In the film, the man looks much healthier than today. He has flesh on his bones, yet already there seemed a gaunt, stark stare to his eyes. He looks dead too.

The documentary follows him in his profession as a performer of autopsies. In one scene, he cracks open the rib cage of a cadaver and looks inside, saying:

"You see. There is no soul inside. Just meat."

He also runs a side-line in directing and producing pornography with teenage boys he picks up at the train station and pays money to have sex on camera.

"Now, up there, everything is covered in pigeon shit. I want you to roll around in the pigeon shit together and fuck each other. It will be hot."

We watch, somewhat aghast, thinking that at times we had lived in the same squat as this man.

Mierda decides to name one of her rats after him.

Despite being dead, I still enjoy the sight of seeing Mierda playing with her rats. She picks up one or both of the soft, squeaking things and presses them to her lips, blowing farts on their bellies and counting their nipples and squealing and laughing and smiling broadly as they run around.

"So soft. So white. So pure. Little lesbo rats!" she would sing to them. I wasn't so sure about them, but she insists and I find myself loosely holding some small, wriggling creature in my hand. It peers at me with pink, blinking eyes, and grips my fingers with weird little human hands – dextrous and nimble. It looks like it could work a typewriter.

On average, about once a week, Mierda lets me fuck her.

"I want to be used," she hisses at me.

But being dead, this all means little to me. I merely exist amongst the living, witnessing what is happening.

"So you end up living with the chaos punks, and they make you be a freak..."

Each time I open the door it feels like the future falls through.

The doorbell of the Shitness School is a repurposed fire bell, painted by Mierda to look like an eyeball exploding out of a seven-foot emaciated zomboid refugee mural painted across one wall. It shrieks like a klaxon announcing trouble, terrors and attacks from outside and a roaring, drunken battle-cry:

"Everybody's an enemy!"

There are refugees from the Vostok – Sasha and Fyodor. A pair of panthers: snake-hipped, dressed to kill, stiletto boys, in heels and with flick knifes in the back pockets, hot-stepping sleuths out of the suburbs of [location redacted]. In top hats and leggings, with a change of clothes for leisure, to shoplift, party or riot, always dressed to the nines and piercing you with the sparky nervous optimism of a person who has slipped the noose, jumped the fence and fled to the woods on the day of execution. Intently on the go, or immersed in a relaxation so intent and focused it could only have been justified by the flight from a state repression much more severe than the TV licence inspector. I knew Fyodor from barricading 27 windows on the front of Squatopolis, where he nearly lost an arm to a bailiff's angle-grinder, and Sasha from his determined razor-sharp patter, cut-throat pragmatism and dapper top hat.

There is dark little Nieszka, small like a collapsed star, of weight and presence beyond her size, squirrelling from mystery to cackling laughter, shrewd and sleek like some magical mole that had burrowed into the squat. From the right angle, she looks like a 12-year old boy. She is the inverse embodiment of the Russian doll with a black mask Mierda had tattooed on to the back of her leg in Squatopolis beneath the words "Matryoshka Riot".

When the Oval squat of over 100 people is evicted, I open the door to a hydra of piercings and shaved areas, tattoos and leather, cheeky grins and glinting eyes: the brothers Daigas and Ratai, and his girlfriend Lice, fresh back from driving across the States, tearing from one coast to the other in a relentless white-line odyssey. I never see Daigas without his vaporiser, a bemused slant to whole being as he staggers in a cannabinoid fug, his haircut that of a space-bum three million years from Earth, laughing and chuckling his way through the void. He is always in pain – back, or neck, or kidneys or liver recovering from some earlier time when he was as fully dedicated to chaos inebriation as some of the others in the Shitness. Now, he is a machine – scrubbing pots in a city salad bar by day and blazing weed in his free time – making plans to bust out of squat's waiting room.

Ratai is by all accounts an incorrigible but loveable cunt, so deadpan uncaring with it you couldn't hate him for long. Street-edge not straight-edge, booze and drugs had no interest for him. He is a cyborg, plugging into the variety of high-end bicycles he had accrued in his time as a courier, slicing hawk-like through London's vicious traffic by day and each weekend taking scalps and glory in the illegal street-races they organise around town. He'd blast the same anti-cop Oi! Songs on repeat until you thought you'd lose your mind, lips twisting in a satisfied smile if he saw you break and snap at him.

I am bewildered how Lice could put up with him. I learned she'd been a hardcore oil-quiff dyke before they'd got together. She looks like a 50s pin-up who'd time-travelled forward and become an alt-porn star. Arms scrawled with bootleg freestyle tatts and ears stretched to bursting point, her hair an emerald coiffure, she could smoke and strut and chat with the easy grace of a Devon lass and champion of chat headed to the city. She was head-chef at the same city luncher as Daigas, and shared the same easy feline smile.

Naiad sashays in during the third week, aquamarine dreadlocks and a shaved pate, a map of the world inked on the square of her back and a jangling, jolly demeanour of the seasoned traveller. A Holiday Queen of hitch-hikers, but with a distant innocence she once explained as having experienced brain-death as a baby. The doctors had to jumpstart her brain with needles. She got lost a lot, but never really seemed to mind. She'd travelled the US with the others, but stayed on an extra month to explore alone. As they reunited, they split the limited numbers of rooms with sheets and simply picked alternate corners with the ease of old sailors dividing a deck into berths.

Another pairing I only passed in the doorways, dimly aware of in the heights of the building, but they remained mysterious and somehow apart. The aptly named Pinky is an incongruous blue-eyed blonde with spectacular breasts and a penchant for Justin Bieber, stylishly restrapping her voluminous curves in K-pop tones of carnation, fuchsia, fandango and magenta. Her partner, Bill, always wears a full-cap, slick t-shirt, trainers, seemingly forever at work as a bar-man. In honesty at times we were so packed on top of each other that his absence was a relief, for when he was there he would talk as incessantly as a techno-rig's bass beats.

Awi talked with the relentless logic of a hacker/coder/tinker/spy – effortless, inarguable, unruly, ineffable. Vastly complex yet built on the confounding binary simplicity of 1 and 0. Long and lean with a lazy glare and an intellect like a razor. A walking paradox in his appropriated words. Unreliable, inexcusable, irresistible, with the gift of the gabba and the same merciless relentlessness. If you were spare some time you could lose yourself in his tail stream as he blazed a trail of spontaneous epiphany and communion through the streets in timeless adventure but fuck help you if you had any sane schedule to keep.

"The first time I met George was in the Place. I walked in, we'd just been evicted, and he was in the basement with a golf club, smashing a television to pieces."

"I had a lot of anger to get out. I remember the wood broke straight away, but the 4 iron did pretty well."

"That was such an introduction."

"I used to be furious. I've calmed down since then. That was during the Terrible Christmas, I remember. We ended up snorting lines of coke off juggling knives and blazing the DMT the hippies were cooking in one of the rooms off the main basement. Christmas Eve morning we were all still going, and I realised I had to go to my mum's house. I raged out and headed to the tube, riding it in totally the wrong direction whilst tearing up a copy of the *Evening Standard* and giving the weird eye to the poor morning commuters there. I was the only one who made it home that Christmas."

He was my in – I had met him that sour holiday and stood by him in the midst of roiling carnage. It was him who rang us when we were sat ragged and bewildered in a mouldy furniture store, bringing a wild-eyed Osmond and me to Squatopolis and the mess that ensued. Maybe he owed me, but he took me into the rain-soaked top floor of the Shitness and whilst he wasn't fucking street-skipped nymphs of Shoreditch alternated with me so I could escape the front room.

Diligently, cap in hand, I had gone from one to the other and begged a place to stay.

"I was wondering if it was alright if I stayed awhile. Me and Ari are taking some time. She's going to stay with my old crew."

The response was open, non-committal. In a world of no future, let's just agree to see how it goes.

And over it all, lingering like the rancid arse pollution of a stray dog fed on rough cuts begged from the local Halal butchers, was the name Bezdalius.

"I don't know where the fuck he is. He's either gone completely out of his mind crazy somewhere or he fucking killed himself," Mierda explained, again, seemingly approached as his abandoned mistress, veil painted repeatedly on her face as black and green warpaint.

I'd met him back in Well Furnished, three years before, at a grand and sombre council of all the squatters from across London: hippies from Grow Heathrow and housing activists slumming Camden, art students from Peckham and scumpunx from beyond the Borough, the crust of Brixton and the lunatic fringe of Penge and Catford, all solemnly assembled around a ludicrous 16-piece polished conference table donated the day before, like some insane pirate parliament. At the round check-in, Bezdalius had corpsed, and bedecked in his finest prototechnozombiecannibal garb, he had announced that he was the undercover policeman in the group.

I'd met him again, outside the formidable iron door of the site of Squatopolis, off Brick Lane, just after the Place was evicted. Three sets of black eyes had peered at me with cool and non-committal intellect, a pack of blown-together spikes, teeth and drool. The tallest was Bezdalius, his insectoid head shaved into a monk-cut, a GG Allin cat-whisker moustache like wispy mandibles above a paralysed sneer like that of a stroke-victim. He was pushing a trolley laden with trash and wearing a home-made breastplate, stencilled with the words "Gas Chambers For Squatters".

Whilst living in Squatopolis, I remember returning home with a bag of sweaty skip, and finding him graffing a huge piece on to one wall: the squat logo being smashed with a fist surrounded by the words "Better Let Homes Rot Than Squat". I'd proudly unleashed a cavalcade of pies and veg and pizza and whatnot and presented it to him.

He'd fixed me deadpan and intoned in a flatline baritone:

"I kind of gave up on food."

But that first time, it wasn't him I had been worried about. Beside him, glittering in the drizzle that first night, was a long, lean German Shepherd with a thick shaggy coat of sienna and jet, straining eagerly on a leash and staring at me with a look that seemed half delirium and half gnostic frenzy. I instinctively froze, two years of living in the mountains with packs of wild dogs teaching me to show no fear, but to hold my ground and observe, unshaken, but aware. The dog barked, and then she barked. It was like a drill sergeant commanding attention, the ragged boom tearing from her throat and echoing down the hollow masonry of Shoreditch into the night sky.

"Grizzly! *Ateik čia!*"

She had lean athletic legs bare in the rain, sprouting from rotten boots with the soles flapping off, crowned with a mane of green and black dreadlocks held back in a sports cap tagged with the word RIOT scrawled across it. Her eyes were painted solid black, with three-black stripes slashed across a cheek, and reams of silver hanging from her ears and lips. She eyed me unblinking, stoic, unreadable. I recognised her from the description Osmond had given me of the belt of Mercedes Benz trophies slung like a bandolier about her defiant hips.

"Hiya. I'm George."

"Mierda." Her voice was deep as a grave.

"George."

They stared. Grizzly parked. I had felt that a fist-bump or handshake might be met with nothing more than those withering stares. I blinked first.

In the choking summer we commence one long, singular frenzy. Our windows open on to Shoreditch High Street, directly opposite the Drunken Monkey. We systemically turn our front room into an anteroom of mindless hedonia. A monolithic speaker parks permanently in front of the open window, the distorted beats relentless, beckoning Shoreditch's sleazy sparkly deities in to join us. Flashes and fragments remain: it opens with the end of one indulgence, after I shyly join Mierda in playful decoration of the hallway – her completing her nightmarish shitcore doorbell golem and me scrawling childish anarchic plagiarisms opposite like a finger-painting special-needs child in rebellion at school. Late in a booze-soaked night the front room suddenly clears, and only we remain, her reclining leopardine and easy on the mattress dumped in one corner, my occasional bed when Awi was hosting. She fixes me from across the room with a hungry and unmistakeable gaze.

A wet kiss and we spill ferally into her room, a tangle of limbs and greedy eyes on to the foam cast on her floor. We pull off each other's clothes, and with satisfying delight I uncover her hidden piercings and the feel of metal and flesh in my hands. She takes me into her mouth, her eyes closing as her studded tongue savours vegan meat. Impatient, I pull her legs apart and push inside her, for a few moments drinking in the rapture on her face as she rolls her zombie grey eyes up into her head.

Too soon, it becomes like pushing rope. The alcohol and the

pressure cause a spectacular fail.

"Ah shit. I'm too drunk to get it up."

"Don't worry, it's normal."

And I knew it was.

The next morning, we blearily wake.

"You made me break my rule."

"What was that?"

"Not to fuck anyone I live with. I need to go to 56a to fix my bike. Maybe you want to come with me," she asked as she pulled on her leggings.

"OK."

The door opens. Her wheeling her busted bike, in the dazzling sunlight of summer, heading south to the Elephant.

"I don't even know where you are from."

"Montenegro."

"Montenegro really? I've never met anyone from there. What's it like?"

She pins me with those cobalt eyes that had rolled up in her skull the night before, betraying nothing.

"I don't identify with any country."

We stroll and talk of something and nothing, and every half a kilometre or so she pauses, and asks if I want a drink, before disappearing into a Tesco's and returning with a liberated bottle of Cobra, a can of Stella, a mischievous twist on her pouting lips.

"Shit. You can really lift."

"I fucking had to learn man. When I first moved here I didn't have shit. I couldn't get a bank account for three months. People had to feed me, or I had to skip food, or I had to steal."

At the bike shop, I sit and leaf through the zine library in the sun, whilst she tinkers and chats and repairs her bike. Once fixed, we saddle up and set off back through the low-rise estates. As we hit Newington Butts, I have a bold moment.

"Do you want to go somewhere to take a shower?"

"OK."

The Shitness doesn't have a working toilet, beyond the shameful triangle jig-sawed into the floor, let alone a shower. People are pinch-arse trailing down to the Boxpark to take a dump.

Now lightning fast and suddenly agile atop the bikes, we roll over to Lambeth North, to where my friend's box flat is nestled in a sleepy village-like backroad. I still have the key from when I was couch surfing there, before being asked to move on. I know his work times, and slipping the Yale I smuggle her in and sordidly up the stairs like an illicit mistress.

"Are you hungry?"

"I kind of gave up on food."

I heat her some tomato soup that she thankfully slurps, and then without much ceremony we strip, clambering into the shower together and tenderly, naturally cleaning ourselves and each other like shaven monkeys grooming.

Afterwards, she wraps a towel coyly around herself.

It lasts only a few minutes before those eyes compel me to peel it from her, and we fuck on the sofa like screeching otters until I shoot my load over her belly button piercing. She quickly showers again before we return home.

Once back, she turns, perfunctorily thanks me and leaves to her room as if nothing had ever transpired. There was no question of there ever being anything more.

Damp and mould and misery rot my lungs. On quieter nights I lay alone on sofa cushions on the top floor being beaten up by my own thoughts. The limited cache of Valium I had left after Amsterdam soon vanishes, and I find myself desperately scrolling through my address book, looking for someone, anyone to text, call, contact. At the chilling sober hours before dawn, with no one to reach out to, I stagger back down to the front room to seek any sort of company to distract me from myself. When it rains I move the cushions further away from the spreading damp across the floor.

In the days, I walk from Shoreditch down Brick Lane to Bethnal Green where there is a taxi cab office with a one-pound internet cafe in the back. Amidst online gamblers and people making braying hilarious Skype calls to distant lands, I sink my mouldy misery into drafting the book, ploughing a couple of hours each day into the expanding chapters, lost in the past five years and trying to do justice to what once was. After a few hours, I buy wine, rewarding myself with capitalism, and walk home to drink until I don't feel anymore.

"So you had sex with Mierda?"

August and Ari is back from Germany, and is to be installed with the remnants of my old crew at the post office I had opened with them in Holloway. I had been steeling myself for it, yet when she came to visit, somehow it all went wrong.

Nurse Dre is round one night, hunting Fyodor and slipping codeine to everyone with a devilish glint. She had been in the ill-fated gym occupation in Stoke Newington too – the place where I had first returned to after India imploded, eating Valium and running 20 miles on the treadmill whilst chanting militaristic squat drills. The place had been a woman-only spa and had a lime-green watered pool on the side of which Fyodor, Sasha and their friends had set up their extensive musical equipment to play endless doom metal. She giggles and says how one night she had come down to see Mierda hooking up with Spike in a secret alcove. I'd smiled at it. The gym had been a self-destructive overture to my return. I couldn't judge – the same week Ari had burst indignantly into the sauna to find me and another male deliriously blowing each other amidst the steam.

"This is not what we agreed."

"Why not just join in Ari? Or close the door – you're letting the heat out."

I know now how Valium not only kills emotion, but seriously

impedes thought. My arrogant maleness, or misguided chauvinism, had led me one night in the Shitness to confide in Spike about my adventure with Mierda. He'd been hanging around for days on some hidden agenda. I didn't understand the ovine horror on his face then, but the next day the text messages began.

"What the fuck. Spike just texted me saying he wants to burn me, and then throw me out a window."

Mierda flails in the front room. "Fucking hell this guy he's been texting me all this shit about how I'm his best friend and he wants to move to India to live up a mountain with me and live on a farm with a sheep and a goat. For fuck's sake, is he like your best friend or something? I fucking woke up in the gym and his hands were already on me. I didn't realise he was a fucking maniac."

Nieszka nodded. "I've had to kick him out of here two times already. He's always just hanging around."

August 7th, and I agreed, half-drunk already, that Ari could visit. It seemed appropriate – before Amsterdam I had missed my bus in the morning and come back to the just-opened Shitness to help her occupy. We had had tortured angry sex on the floor of one room before I fled again that night.

"So you had sex with Mierda?"

Spike had texted her as well, telling her to tell her boyfriend to keep his hands off his woman. It was plenty enough to cause the meeting to descend into the familiar eviscerating pattern of tears and recrimination.

"I just need some space. I just need some fucking space. Leave. Please leave. It's my birthday it's my birthday how can you -"

We simply knocked the scab off of two years of deeply savage misunderstanding. By the time she leaves, I am howling on the roof, four stories up, spitting tears of despair at the distant silver obelisks of the city. I walk down to the ledge and without thinking too much about it, climbed up to balance on the precipice. Mantha is there, calm and present and monastic, awkward with my tears, but refusing to leave.

I wonder then, very calmly, very raw and alive, if I would hit anyone on Shoreditch High Street if I was to take a single step forward. I wonder, in a diamond moment of lucid emptiness, if that was enough of reality for me.

And then my phone beeps. A message. From Mierda.

RU READY FOR SOME PAIN?

I choke a laugh, wipe my eyes and step back.

Heading back through the fire exit, I drop into mine and Awi's dank room and grab the pack of Naproxene and the tabs of acid I was saving for that day, and head down to Mierda's Shitty Tattoo Corner.

For the next few hours, I lie on a purple massage chair beneath a crinkly plastic banner of a beachside scene, a sun lounger lying on sand beneath a palm tree. I lose myself in physical pain and hallucinogenic synaesthesia as Mierda carved the words CREATE and DESTROY into my shoulders. On acid, the pain is giggly and confusing, a cathartic relief from the emotional shitstorm I am so unsuccessfully navigating. Nurse Dre arrived at the end with a bottle of Honey Jack Daniels, and we decide to pierce my nipples.

I wake up on the living room floor, searing pain through my side, and a patch of gaffer tape over my left nipple.

Awi is looming over me, dressed in a tiger onesey.

"Hey buddy. How are you doing?"

I groan and tear the gaffer tape off my nipple, peer at the hole that went through the meat of my tit. Mierda is swanning through, and executes a perfect pirouette with the grace only training can bring.

"Fucking hell man you were on one last night. Dre tried to pierce your nipple. It was all going fine until you moved and twisted at the last minute."

Awi nods. "After that, we found you upside down at the bottom of the stairs. You also nearly fell out the window. You knocked all the plant pots off. The police came to check. We had to keep bringing you back to the sofa and laying you down."

Mierda laughs. "You told them it was a private party. We had to tell everyone to not go anywhere near you. Every time someone touched you you would go off again like a maniac. We were on the brink of tying you up."

I look from one to the other, but in each face saw no judgement, no criticism, despite what they had seen. We all smile together, and off it goes.

The next day I cannot move, and lie comatose but awake for an age on the sofa in the front room whilst Awi and Mierda combat in relentless verbal war on anything and everything, blazed on whisky and each refusing to back down.

"Mierda's a feminist."

"Fucking men and their fucking cocks have fucked up the whole world."

"A vegan feminist."

"Kill all your fucking babies and eat them."

Another morning rises, and Fyodor is with us, laden with shoplifted gin that we pass between us. This morning Awi has brought a slender Nordic girl home with him – only the latest in his incessant plundering of Shoreditch's pliant female visitors. R. was skipped from the street, with elfin hair and a body like a dolphin, but he has passed out on the floor under a blanket. Dre is preparing doses of MDMA which we pass around on a copy of *Into the Volcano,* and when I next turn around, R. and Mierda are passionately kissing. Without pretence, I lean in and intercept to kiss Mierda, our three faces ecstasy warmed, eyes hooded and sublime, and then the three of us together, our tongues dancing three ways. Then, I turn to Fyodor and ask, invite, leaving the girls to enjoy each other more, and then feel the rough of his stubble against my face, his tongue in my mouth.

Mierda keeps saying: "You can sleep in my bed if you like," to R. but she has a "lover boy" and is determined to be good. Still, she sits between us and mine and Mierda's hands have free run of her taut body, discovering she has piercings in hidden places as well.

Another night and I have brought a bottle of red wine with no egg. I realise I need something from my bag, but upon reaching it realise Awi has barricaded himself inside and scrawled "FUCK OFF! NO ENTRY! DO NOT DISTURB!" on the outside. Naturally, after hammering on the door for a while, our collective response is to drill a hole through it with the Makita and shove the nozzle of a fire extinguisher through to undiscriminatingly douse whoever was inside.

When we see him next, all he says is: "You guys are dicks."

Of course the tattoos get infected, crusting over with greenish scab and a dull, syphilitic ache. I begin a regime of kettle-washing in the collapsing kitchen to try to clean them out, constantly concerned the roof may cave in, or the floor fall through. During one night, Fyodor knocks the amplifier over and it crushes my big toe, splitting the nail right down the middle. It would never really grow right again.

Another morning, and we are sat crushing co-codemol and trying to snort it, scarring our noses and livers with paracetamol in a misguided attempt to hit the codeine. Back from work, Bill explains to me as if to a child about cold-pressing it to extract it, about how I've probably poisoned myself, that that's why my side hurts, and it's probably not broken ribs from my birthday but severe liver damage. I don't like Bill at that moment.

Another night and I am reeling on whisky, determined to take Awi to task as a contrarian, to challenge him on the fact that he always has to challenge back, that he can never just accept an argument without countering with another. My rage and frustration builds until I break, tearful, defeated and flee to hide uninvited in Mierda's bed.

"Why are you crying?"

"Because Awi is a fucking dick. And life is fucking futile. And really, because monogamy doesn't work, and all relationships are doomed."

"Well, that's fucking reality. You're born alone, and you die alone, and in the middle you get fucked over a lot. Life is pain. Deal with it. You aren't the only one whose relationship has ended."

"How long were you together?"

"Four years. How long were you and your 'wife' together?"

"Two or three. We were husband and wife in India. They don't really get it any other way out there."

"Fucking wife," she scoffs. "So traditional."

At some point, we are invaded by couriers in lycra and the unwinding easy generosity of the spectacularly tired. Raitus and I tag team playing ska, Oi and 2-tone for an evening's relief from Mierda's violent shitcore noise beats and Awi's frankly ridiculous garage and chatter. We compete for the longest run of anti-cop songs in a row. They dish out Guinness and babble about bikes and dockets and controllers, equal parts exhausted and relieved, and it's great to be entertained.

I cry a lot at bus-stops, spontaneously collapsing into the timetables scheduling the 294, just another soul overwhelmed by public transport. People ignore me.

Other random punks drop in, and old friends visiting, and ever more wild-eyed tourist girls for Awi to fuck on the roof, and the volume of the place is never less than cacophonic. One evening I awake on the front sofa between Mierda and some rent-a-punk from some fucking town full of wankers, and we do a line of speed together before I have to head north to Holloway and the post office squat where Ari now lives with A. and Pidge and Dre to collect a shit bike from Ari.

"This speed has made me really horny," I confess.

Meeting Ari again is a predictable nightmare of resentment and rage. After an hour of trying to simply have a nice time with A. and my old friends, I flee on the piece of shit bike they found in there, intentionally abandoned as part of a barricade, creaking and squealing and groaning all the way back south like fleeing the scene of a crime. Before arriving, I flip the bike on to its back outside a Sainsbury's and rage through, stuffing a Cobra into my jacket as a gift for Mierda. Triumphant and relieved I sweep back into the front room, to find it empty.

I knock on her door.

"FUCK OFF!"

I text her: I have brought you a present.

Moments later, the punk emerges, pulling on his t-shirt and heading to the misery-hole toilet. He has an ACAB tattoo on his inner arm. Mierda emerges after, and I give her the beer.

There is a pause as we both stand, expressing silence, feeling a threshold.

"Did you have sex with him?"

She looks at me, and there is a crack of sympathy in the mask of her make-up as she barely, almost imperceptibly nods. I turn and head back to my lonely miserable room. There is nothing more to say.

A week later, T. sets me up with a girl from her work, and I apply Awi's patented method of a whirlwind alcohol-soaked tour through the alleyways of East London, culminating in a rooftop date of the squat. When we arrive, Awi is already squeezed with some giggling girl in one corner, so I escort my date down to our room. We lie down on the damp sofa cushions, and I push myself through the near-crippling pain of my broken ribs to awkwardly, unenthusiastically fuck, afterwards collapsing back barely able to breathe whilst she encouragingly sucked on my defeated cock.

"I think I'm going to call a taxi."

"OK."

She didn't leave a number.

The dead get fucked and chucked, failures at being stiff in the right places.

But being dead, such things do not really matter. I am determined despite the agony and the savage collapse of my dreams to not repeat my pattern of falling directly into another doomed, misguided relationship. I write. I drink. I steal. I am surprised how much the dead suffer. I call up my parents and cry uncontrollably down the phone, just wailing gasping torment as they say "there there". I sit under bridges in the rain. I invite old friends over and show them the scat-insanity of our toilet, the rain pouring through the kitchen. I sign on at Crisis, joining the weekly Wing Chun workshops, which Mierda laughingly called "bum fu", warning me about all the diseases I risk getting fighting in the hobo dojo.

And then, the court papers arrived.

The dead also get evicted.

3

From Paris, With Rage

Nonviolence declares that the American Indians could have fought off Columbus, George Washington, and all the other genocidal butchers with sit-ins; that Crazy Horse, by using violent resistance, became part of the cycle of violence, and was "as bad as" Custer. Nonviolence declares that Africans could have stopped the slave trade with hunger strikes and petitions, and that those who mutinied were as bad as their captors; that mutiny, a form of violence, led to more violence, and, thus, resistance led to more enslavement. Nonviolence refuses to recognize that it can only work for privileged people, who have a status protected by violence, as the perpetrators and beneficiaries of a violent hierarchy.
Peter Gelderloos, *How Nonviolence Protects the State*

Cops with eyes like sharks and faces like the underside of a boot are waiting for us as we get off the bus from London – the state of emergency manifest as a column of cyborg *gendarmerie* toting an arsenal of machineguns, tasers, handcuffs and kevlar armour. They stare. We stare back – predator and prey eyeing each other before the chase commences. We slip past them unmolested, disappearing into the suffocating warmth of the Metro. I am glad to be travelling with a trio of giggly matronly types. They are three women from EcoDharma, attendees of the first theatre of the oppressed workshop I gave there two months before: Oak – a bright-eyed leprechaun with fiery red hair and ruddy cheeks, their chuckling demeanour masking deep sensitivity and a scarred heart; Z. a shaven headed elfin with a smile like a new moon, currently living in an intentional community in the south of Spain; Susannah – long, viridian tresses and a crackling voice, visiting out of Bristol and at the biggest protest she's been to in her 70 years.

"Ha. You're like the virgin, the crone and the mother."

"I'm no mother."

"I'm no virgin."

"And who you calling a crone?"

They laugh, a harmony like a deer bursting through dry twigs to crash into a babbling brook, echoing unnatural against the tiles of the Metro. They haven't stopped talking the whole trip over from London.

The benches of the Parisian boulevards are lined with huddled forms in sleeping bags, their possessions arranged neatly around them like genteel barricades. It's warm down here, even peaceful once the trains stop running.

Still, I am relieved we have the promise of a roof, of a bed and shelter.

We march, and arrive at L'Annexe only to discover everyone has already moved on to a cabaret night at another squat. We troupe over there, a long walk through dark city streets.

Two bullet holes in a window with an unhappy smiley face painted below them form macabre eyes to the frown. I am reminded of Budapest, where my guide pointed them out in the walls of the buildings from the revolutionary days.

"God," says Oak. "Is this where the shooting was?"

"One of the places," says Z.

We cast our eyes over the layers of floral tributes laid out before La Belle Equipe. Hundreds of bouquets, handwritten messages, candles, roses, lilies, tulips, some faded and shrivelled already, others freshly dropped, lying piled on the ground, stacked before the closed doors of the restaurant.

Z. is chattering. I catch only the second half of it: "-there was also the have-nots, the economic underclass who attended no cabarets, whose labour built the tower. There was even a gang of illegalist anarchist bank robbers around at that time in France – the Bonnot Gang – who stole from banks calling it expropriating from the rich. They were the first people to use motorcars to getaway. The police had to chase them on foot or on bicycles. They started after the leader was fired by his boss -"

"You have to ask – would they have started robbing banks if there had been work for them?"

"God, I wonder," asks Oak. "I wonder how many waiters, *plongeurs* and busboys died in the shooting?"

"Is it better that the rich die than the poor?" asks Z.

"I'm tired. Let's go to bed," says Susannah.

L'Annexe is impressive: a tall, four-floor warehouse complex, scrubbed clean and polished, carpeted and furnished. It reminds me of all the best social centres from London, and like them it will only be short-lived. Opened by a crew who thought they were about to be evicted, they remained in their old home and volunteered the space to host its arts-activism programme during the COP21 Climate Conference.

I drift through the kitchen area, where hot soup and salad is being prepared by members of the Anti-Cop Kitchen Collective, through a partition of plastic sheeting, past a serious sounding meeting on food rights and conscious cafés in South America. There is bustle and business everywhere, the place a hive of activity.

"So hello, this is the legal briefing. Thanks for attending. Now as you are going to be part of the de-escalation team, you will be at high-risk of violence and arrest as you will be stood directly between the police lines and the main protest. It's important that you memorise the names of some solicitors who are sympathetic to the cause, as the police will think you intended to be arrested if you write the names or the numbers down on your body. They will not call the number off the flier.

"At the refugee march, people attended and were then later identified and arrested by the police at other events. This is because of the state of emergency. Fifty-eight people were arrested, yet only two received warnings for attending a forbidden demo. Maximum sentence for this is one year imprisoned.

"At the Climate march there was a mass act of civil disobedience that resulted in a kettle, tear gas and baton charges and 317 random arrests.

"You don't have to carry your ID. You can give your name and a date of birth, and that counts as identifying yourself, but you may want to decide whether you wish to comply with the police state. If they don't believe you, you want to prepare that someone has access to your passport. You could be asked to leave France for one year.

"If you are attending the march, you need to plan as if you will get arrested. If you are taking a gas mask, it is classed as a defensive weapon. You should be careful taking anything that could be deemed a projectile. Don't take any drugs, knives, guns or whatever, and if you are arrested, try to hide your phone inside your pants, as the police here don't check as thoroughly as other places. There's already been examples of people uploading video messages from inside the jail. If you're caught, call the number and tell them which police station you are in."

"So what have the police said about the march?"

"It changes every day. Under the state of emergency it's illegal for more than two people with a political message to gather, which is why people are heading to the convergence point in pairs. Any attendance at a political protest is an act of civil disobedience. They have permitted the human chain and tolerated writing 'climate justice' with people's bodies. The protest with the thousands of empty pairs of shoes was beautifully done, but the red-lines action is still civil disobedience. The state of emergency means more stop and search and raids on many of the squats and convergence centres across Paris. L'Annexe was raided just last week by a hundred stormtroopers and is under constant armed surveillance. We are half expecting another raid before Saturday. The legal team for the protests have been put under house arrest, but nothing more.

"If you are arrested, you need to use the buddy system. Make sure you are clear who your buddy is, and do not lose them. If they go to the toilet, you go with them. With your buddy you organise into an affinity group, making sure you are always with people who are watching, but not at risk. They should always know who is there, what happened, and where, and afterwards these are the guys who greet you outside the police station with champagne.

"Now, please can you raise your hands, wrists together. If you bend your hands down, when they put the handcuffs on you they will be looser than if you just keep your hands like this. Believe me, if you are cuffed for a long time, this will make a big difference. Remember to hide your phone in your pants and when you can, smuggle it out and text people to let them know what's happened to you. The process at the station is that they will fingerprint you, photo you and frisk you, but not very thoroughly. Often at this point it's easy to 'accidentally' smudge the fingerprints, or mess up the photo somehow, or generally play around with them to delay a bit more. They will keep you for four hours to ID check, then up to 24 hours to investigate you.

"When you are to be released, you don't have to sign anything. Repeat – YOU DO NOT HAVE TO SIGN ANYTHING. They may pressure you, but there are people already regretting signing something they did not really understand, and it's making more problems for them now. Even when you receive your possessions back, you do not have to sign anything. Repeat – YOU DO NOT HAVE TO SIGN ANYTHING. The police may put something else in with your stuff and cause you a lot of problems. Some people we know unwittingly signed a conditional discharge, and if they had held out, they wouldn't have had to sign anything.

"They normally tell you it's a piece of paper describing your time in custody, but the translators there are very much on the police's side. If they do anything illegal during your time in custody, you can appeal afterwards, but if you sign, it makes it much, much harder.

"If you have no access to a lawyer or interpreter, try to keep mental notes on what the police do, or do not do, and make physical notes immediately afterwards. If the police decide they are going to investigate a crime, they will give you access to a solicitor within four hours.

"Now, when being interviewed, it's a bit different from in the UK. In France it is not 'no comment', but 'I have nothing to declare'. Repeat after me."

"I HAVE NOTHING TO DECLARE."

"Again."

"I HAVE NOTHING TO DECLARE."

"Again!"

"I HAVE NOTHING TO DECLARE!"

"Now let me describe my ideal arrest. I'm in for 24 hours, so I can rest, I am with my friends. I have done the handcuff trick so I am 'comfortable', and have my phone hidden in my pants. I've told them I have nothing to declare, and have managed to smudge my fingerprints and ruin the photo. I sign nothing! After 24 hours I am released with my friends and greeted by champagne and chocolate and beer.

"Now, afterwards, I have to deal with trauma. Arrests can be and are often violent. I need to make sure that I have money for the Metro, a map. The police could release me somewhere far away where I've never been before. Have you got a safe, warm place to go back to? A major thing after release is not to pressure people, give them time. At some point they will want to speak.

"Make sure you take the time to read all the legal info, educate yourself as much as possible.

"So overall, gatherings are prohibited. You can get a maximum fine of 75,000 Euros or six months in prison, but so far all that has been issued is a warning. They have the power to ban people from certain areas, or force certain groups to dissolve.

"Let's talk about medical preparation. Tear gas. First of all, it's a projectile weapon. If you get hit by a canister it can seriously hurt. It can kill. Secondly, the gas burns on the skin, the eyes, but it won't kill you. It's like intensely concentrated onions, but it won't kill you, so don't panic. You can limit its effect with a scarf soaked in vinegar or lemon juice. Make sure you have baby wipes. Now if tear gas is blowing in the wind, walk upwind of it, sideways. Unless of course the police are there. There's some great footage from the 29th if any of you are into riot porn.

"If it gets on to your skin, it can cause some problems. Don't wear any make-up, and wear glasses, not contact lenses, as they can melt into the eye. If it's CS gas you may not even see it, as it's invisible. Now can I have a volunteer to pretend they've been tear-gassed? Ok, thank you.

"Now, if I see someone has been gassed, what do I do? Ok, calm down, calm down, it's ok. It's Eve here. Kneel down, turn your head on one side. And now I squirt water in from one side. Now, from the other. Good. If you do it from the top down it can burn the body. Tell them the effects won't last more than half an hour.

"Pepper spray is a short-range weapon. If it gets on the clothes, remove them. When you go home, don't have a hot shower, wipe it off and use cold water."

"It helps to have clean skin."

"One day I might."

"I once saw someone in tear gas stand with their eyes screwed shut and not move. Just before it hit, they took a huge deep breath, hyperventilated and waited until it subsided, sipping air with their eyes closed."

"Swimming goggles can also help. One of the hardest things is the impulse to get away. We ended up fumbling around with our buddies.

"Ok, now if the police charge, one more thing is to cover your head and neck with your hands. If you want to keep your hands up, make sure you do so in fists not fingers as the batons will smash them to pieces...

"Ok, let's review the solicitor names..."

"The struggle is the tension between holding on and letting go."

We are in the large space downstairs at l'Annexe. Word of the workshop has spread. I count 60 people lined up against one wall. An expectant, almost religious silence has descended. Even towards the other half of the space, beyond the plastic curtains I can see people tip-toeing past as they continue to prepare the next meal from the Anti-Cop Kitchen.

I swallow and breathe deep down into my stomach in short, controlled bursts.

This is a totally spontaneous, open exercise. I have never done it with so many people.

"The ritual. We are going to perform a ritual together. When I say begin, you are invited to enter into the space and perform your part of the ritual. The ritual will be over when it is over. There will be no set time-limit. When we collectively feel it has come to a close, it will be over. The world needs healing. We need healing. So this shall be a ritual of healing."

There is a long, open moment, and for that moment my heart leaps into my throat and my stomach clenches and my mind whirls and my tongue goes dry.

"Begin."

At first in silence, people begin to move, entering into the space, prostrating themselves on the floor, or beginning to walk in slow circles. At first, the efforts are individual, chaotic, fragmented invitations, but then the machine mind takes over, and people begin to connect and feel what is happening around them, to move together cohesively. No one speaks. No one explains or directs or orders. People sense and feel how to work together to create this ritual space spontaneously, without pre-planning, without leaders or followers, people coming together autonomously to create something bigger than their individual selves.

A bald-head monk in saffron robes is moving in slow, serene circles around the outside, chanting low and calm. Others join him, breaking from smaller circles within to follow. A second circle, closer in, is faster and lighter, people skipping and singing in high clear voices, whirling their arms and zigzagging high and low like swallows on the evening breeze. At the centre, dead centre, a woman kneels, head to the crowd, piercing the chanting and song with a high-pitched, keening wail.

Others gather to her, and the lamentations sear through the room, high, screeching releases of treble agony, soaring above the mid-level melodies and the deep, bass chanting.

The room is electrified. I feel every nerve on my body tingle. A hallucinogenic harmony swamps the space. Time dissipates and I have visions of the entire solar system, the Spiral Arm of the galaxy, whirling in cosmic union in this room in Paris. Electron people whirl around atoms of raw emotion in human form. My head swims with the mix of chanting, wailing and shattering whoops.

And then the movement begins to slow, person by person, sections of the mandala settling to rest, contemplative and still. Frequency by frequency, silence is restored. A stillness settles over the group, part by part, until everything is frozen and there is only the deafening emptiness of 60 people breathing together.

My voice rumbles as if in a cavern.

"The ritual is now at an end. You may remain in this space if you wish, or you may leave. If you need people, reach out to those around you. Take care of yourself. Thank you."

Trancelike and wild-eyed, people drift from the mandala, and it crumbles apart as people silently and slowly return to themselves. Ambient noise of the kitchen, the street, the world returns.

"Fooking hell," says Oak. "That were a bit intense, want it?"

I've been invited to sit in with Rooty, Eve and M., who gave the legal briefing earlier in the day. We gather upstairs in one of the open workspaces. People drift through. Looking round the three women, it seems like they have been barely sleeping for weeks. They have all been here more than a month, organising and participating, working ceaselessly to coordinate the many different groups involved in the protest. It seems they have a job for me.

"So we've been tasked with this de-escalation...We are now de-escalation angels. But is it even really possible?"

"We've been in almost constant contact with the police, and with the Secretary of State. They are terrified that tomorrow will turn into a riot. I mean, is this going to work?"

"Well, as I see it, the de-escalation crew's role is to help create a joyous atmosphere. We'll be public game playing, some stewarding I guess, and generally trying to help turn tense situations around and have fun. If the tear gas goes off we've obviously already failed."

"So the Rebel Clown Army will be there. They will be on the front line next to the police, then you guys, and then the main march. Also, the Climate Angels will be coming, have you seen them? Oh they are just amazing, with these huge, feathered wings. Just beautiful. There's a great video online of a wing smacking a cop in the face – purely by accident of course. There's going to be foghorns announcing the beginning of the march, the moment when people lay the flowers down, and then two minutes silence."

"At the end of the two minutes silence the brass band will kick off, and the party starts."

"So we're really going for a funeral ritual. A funeral for the environment, for the failure of the governments to do anything meaningful, and then a big party atmosphere."

"I can't wait for Saturday night when it's all over. I am going to do some serious dancing."

"Straight out of the cells and on to the dance floor, ha ha."

"It's been a long two weeks."

"We've all earned it."

"Oh, the workshops today just helped so much. So much relief, just to remember that all of this is just made up. Invented."

"It's so easy to get sucked into all the bullshit, but that's really all it is."

"We can tell you now what the route is going to be -"

"But that might all change -"

"Again. We're on to like Plan X."

"It's been a constant clusterfuck. Any other changes – and there will be I'm sure – and we will inform everyone through text. Make sure people get their numbers down for the tree."

"But as of tonight the convergence will be at the Arc de Triomphe."

"And from there march to the Eiffel Tower."

"So the police, the government are all terrified of anything happening to the Arc de Triomphe. Any vandalism. As much as a bottle thrown at it. They will charge."

"They will charge. I mean you couldn't have a bigger symbol of nationalism, militarism, of France itself."

"They have elections in Paris this weekend and they're terrified of a riot. They say if there's a riot, the Right will win in the elections."

"It'll ruin the Left's reputation."

"By the way, what do you think? Should we buy plant pots for tomorrow?"

"Plant pots?"

"Yes. For the tear gas. It's the best way to contain it apparently. You just pop a plant pot over the top."

"Errr…Better to have them and not need them I suppose."

Suddenly Z. arrives, tears in her eyes, but laughing at the same time.

"I just found out my boyfriend slept with someone else."

"That's not funny. Why are you laughing?"

"Oh no, are you ok?"

"Yeah, I know. Just now. I mean, it's annoying. It's a shock. I mean, he was the one who didn't want a polyamorous relationship. He said he was really drunk, and that he hadn't been drunk like that in over a year."

"That's really no excuse."

"Oh love, come here."

"Don't worry, we'll look after you. It's going to work out."

"Thanks, guys. Sorry. Let's get back to the meeting."

"So the coalition has agreed that we will not cross the police lines. If we do, they will charge and shut the whole thing down. If anything is thrown, a single thing, they will charge. We've gotten all the different groups to agree to the nonviolence policy. It's been a massive job."

"One of the clowns knows the black bloc crew and he's meeting with them tonight to ask them not to attend this march."

"Black bloc here is a bit different than from in the UK. In the UK, they tend to turn up, join in a march, get a bit rowdy, and that's it."

"The guy said here 'they take it seriously'."

"Whatever that means. Anyway, so hopefully they won't be there. They can do their own thing, somewhere else, all power to them, but not here."

"It's all going to be super-fluffy."

"We hope. After the 29th the last thing we need is another load of arrests and tear gas."

"The police are going to do everything they can to avoid that."

"Maybe tomorrow we could schedule sometime for you to talk directly to the de-escalation bloc. A few of them were a bit shocked by the legal briefing. I think it all got a bit real for them, talking about tear gas and smashed hands and jail."

"It's all really unlikely, but of course, everyone should be as prepared as possible for what could happen."

"One woman has permanently affixed contact lenses. She's terrified they are going to melt into her eyes! But tomorrow, yes, we'll organise the group more directly and get everyone to assess where they are comfortable being on the day."

"God, I'm just so tired…"

"Don't worry, we are nearly there now."

We set about our plan, preparing to hit the streets the next day as a human buffer, part of a layer cake of defence between 20,000 protesters, the Rebel Clown Army and the delightful French riot police.

We speed-date people in pairs to find their buddy. They circle through a number of potential dates, discussing their willingness to be near The Front, as it is known. They discuss fears, hopes, expectations, before swirling on.

I partner with a smiling young bearded Worcestershire boy named J. – another volunteer from EcoDharma.

"Every buddy pair, get with the buddy pair next to you, so you are a four. This is your brick. Stay close to your brick as much as possible. You are two pairs of buddies, looking after each other. If one half gets arrested, the other can report it. Get their numbers now."

I sidle over to Oak as the group begins to disperse. She is smiling excitedly, and has buddied with Z., who also grins expectantly. My buddy J. gathers too. This is our brick. We do a group hug, linking our arms around one another.

"So," I say. "Ready for a riot?"

An iceberg from Greenland has been dragged to Paris by boat, where it now sits outside the Pantheon in more than a dozen gleaming shards of diamond, decaying infinitesimally and inexorably before our eyes. We walk, humbled, mesmerised, touching each one solemnly, the icy water chilling our fingertips, anointing our foreheads with it. I wonder how many thousands of years these droplets of water had been trapped in the ice, how many lives had passed between now and the last time it existed as a liquid, how many moments had been strung in between. The scale of it is overwhelming. At the head of our procession, a Buddhist monk in saffron robes with a gentle American English accent provides some reassurance in his quiet confidence, a timely reminder of the inherent emptiness of all phenomena, allowing some philosophical perspective on the tragedy of ecocide.

I have already linked up with J.; the other buddies and bricks arrive in discreet pairs, having been told to spread out to avoid arousing suspicion. There is Rooty and her wife Loupe, Susannah and the monk, Eve, Z. and Oak. Everywhere are the bright flashes of red we have been asked to wear as part of the red-lines protest.

"Freedom, freedom, freedom…Freedom on my mind."

The song spreads, voices raised in the simple refrain, voices harmonising, male and female and other, high and low.

It feels faintly ridiculous, all this hippie trash, but it helps people relax.

Eventually, in that strange group-mind telepathy, silence descends, broken by the ululating cries of a wedding taking place in the church opposite. We return the cry joyously, releasing more tension, more stress, up into the clear Parisian sky.

A tall man in a dog-collar and white suit, his hair a silvery bouffant crown of steel wool, steps from the circle to address us in a strong, mercurial tone.

"Brothers and sisters can I get an Earth-a-llujah?"

"Earth-a-llujah!"

"Amen, brothers and sisters. My name is the Reverend Billy,

of the Church of Stop Shopping. I'm from New York City, and for many years now, myself and members of the congregation of the Choir of Stop Shopping have been travelling around, meeting with like-minded individuals and preaching the Gospel of Stop Shopping. We are wild, anti-consumerist Gospel shouters and Earth-loving urban activists who have worked with communities all over the world defending community, life and imagination.

"It's an honour to be here in Paris, and to have attended the workshop yesterday and seen such powerful moments of healing, of people coming together, to nurture each other, to heal one another. Can I get an Earth-a-llujah?"

"EARTH-A-LLUJAH!"

"This week we've seen some dancing in the streets. In particular, the dance with police is heart-breaking and revealing. It is a gift to all of us out here who will carry on the Earth's work, the job of tornado-ing in the plazas. The mind-leap that the politicians and police make – that any gathering in public space resembles the Other and must be called Extreme – this doesn't seem like France, but I am naive.

"My lazy thinking has it that I myself would never be this way, but we all fall back into fear, don't we? We are the predator species, and we forget that we are made of the Earth. We are mammals made of soil and ocean-water, a column of water up on our hind legs.

"That is what we are on both sides of the conflict. But one side has a club and no face. The other, you, you bring your vulnerable body as close to the action as you dare. You show your flesh to the public air and receive the bruise. You show a smile, you are hopping in place, and then running back to slow down a friend's arrest. Can I get an Earth-a-llujah?"

"EARTH-A-LLUJAH!"

"When we protest we make a storm in the street that the Earth's horizon watches with interest. The Earth is our leader and our teacher. We know that the Earth will win. She will heat up but she will survive the extinction that sweeps across her eco-systems. We know that the men in body-armour will join us ultimately as we fall to the ground like leaves in the autumn. At some point the cops too will feel the Earth in their bodies – that is what will persuade them not to work for nationalism descended from old wars.

"The Earth fills us up and sends us into the fight with instructions in its singing molecules. She gives us power beyond policies, ego or courage.

"When we watch you on the streets we feel a strange kind of gratitude – your bodies are like letters arranging in words against the page of the ground. You give us our new instructions!

"Now I don't have my choir here with me, but two sisters here have volunteered to lead us in a song, Sisters, if you could?"

Two of the sisters step forward.

"This is a song we heard at the conference a lot, a lot of the young activists were singing it during some of the actions, like the Louvre oil action, and I think it's great that we pick up the voices of others. It goes like this...:

People gonna rise like the water, gonna turn this crisis round.
Hear the voice of my great-grand-daughter, singing Climate Justice Now.

We sing between the icebergs and below the Pantheon, and I remember that this is completely illegal, no more than two people are allowed to gather for a "political purpose" under the state of emergency. As our merry troupe of fluffy rainbow-hippies sing I can't help but think what utter nonsense that is. I imagine clouds of tear gas pop-pop-popping as canisters fly. I imagine us all crushed and fleeing beneath a charge of black-clad robocops.

I am sat on a bridge overlooking the lazy snake of the Seine as it swirls below me, the free curry and rice given away by garishly dressed hippies from huge steel pots sitting like foam on the water of a sewage outlet in my stomach. My mouth is dry, parched, and all around me herds of strange animals drift and wander: people carrying signs that read "system change not climate change", a pod of merpeople, their hair sea-green with plastic seaweed, a knot of chic students wearing keffiyehs and aviators, a single clown with a white face and red nose holding a balloon in the shape of a heart.

Below me, the brass band is lounging, a mob of 20 people in pink shirts and scarves, lounging in the baking sun, their brass instruments sparkling next to them like the weapons of ornamental soldiers. They have been parping and blasting for the last few hours, the strains of *Bella Ciao* still ringing in my ears from the assembly in front of the Arc de Triomphe.

Ahead, the Eiffel Tower rises, a monumental spear of iron matrices shooting into a cerulean sky. The walkways around it are a sea of waving flags and banners, people choking every spot of land with colour and movement, swirling in and around each other. Currently on the bridge, a number of people have chosen to sit down and symbolically block the path, urged on by a manic young man with a megaphone. For now, the police are observing casually, seemingly counting under their breath before intervening. I have no energy left, and drift off towards the tower to find the others.

J. falls in beside me, a gentle, calming presence, passing me a bottle of water.

"So. What do you think?"

I cast my mind back as we walk. The police had been waiting for us at the Arc de Triomphe. I had been searched by a cop with a face like dogshit. He had found nothing, though he made me remove my leather gloves with studs on them that I had worn against the chill.

Once out of the Metro, we had seen that we were walking into a kettle designed to collect us. At the far end of the boulevard, still 100 metres before the Arc, a row of grey battle-buses with lines of armoured cops like legionnaires in front of them, blocking our way. At the opposite end, before the roundabout, a second line had drawn up to prevent us leaving. The side roads were still open, left for us to try to disperse, but it was like walking into a cage.

And thousands of people did walk in. We had assembled, orderly and polite, a sea of red and flags of all nations, colours, banners, people blowing whistles and chanting and cheering: "We are nature defending itself!" The sounds of indigenous pan-pipes interwove with the stamping chants of woad-painted Earth-defenders clutching home-made shields emblazoned with sigils of trees, hawks and turtles, a fettle of people dressed as deep-sea divers, swimming down the street in slow-motion.

At the police line, the dozen or so rebel clowns were already in position, mocking the stance of the cops with their own military pomp. We had lined up behind them, becoming the second buffer line. Whereas the clowns faced the cops, we faced inwards to the sea of people.

The foghorns blasted, and for two minutes, the thousands of people had fallen silent.

I thought about the lake of dead fish I had seen in India where the water had become too acidic from pesticides. I thought about those thousands of glassy-eyed fish washing up on to the shore, and the people from the village gathering to stare incredulously and hopelessly at them.

Then the brass band had fired up, and a great, ragged cheer had gone up from the crowds. The march had begun.

Except the cops had blocked both ways, and there had been no real way for the march to go. They had left open one exit, leading to the left out of the boulevard, and we stood between the clowns and the crowd as thousands of people marched towards us, and as cheerfully as possible we directed them to the left, to squeeze in twos and threes through this narrow gap and continue on their way towards the Eiffel Tower.

It had not felt great, but we stuck to our plan and stayed happy and felt the tension disperse as more and more people fed through the gap. The banners had to be folded up to pass. The Climate Angels, tall, exquisite creatures painted in silver and gold, with huge, ornate, feathery wings of pearl and lapis lazuli, had to edge carefully between the last cop and the wall of the building to get through.

"That boulevard," I was saying to J. as we walked back down the bridge towards the tower. "It was chosen so that nobody would see anything."

We gather up Oak and Z., looking elated but exhausted.

"Well, at least no broken bones, no tear gas!" says Oak. We smile.

Soon we are through the crowds, and directly under the Eiffel Tower, looking upwards at its skeletal innards like tiny teenagers looking up some massive madam's metal skirts. It is dizzying, and we sit down on some benches, feeling deflated.

A woman half-hidden in a scarf, but with cropped blonde hair and piercing blue eyes, drifts lazily past me and hands me a piece of paper. On it is typed:

We are all angry now. As destroyers of the death-reality, we must act. The time for peaceful subjugated protest and failed A to B marches is over. They have made criminals of us all. We call on all those who are willing to gather and express their rage in defence of the Earth. Let us take back the streets and defy the state of emergency.

Meet at Belleville Metro 1900hrs.

I smile.

"Now this looks more like it."

We get out of the Metro one stop early, wary of walking into a trap, and stroll down to Belleville in high spirits. Our brick swaps beers and rolls cigarettes, skipping through the crowds out shopping or leaving work, approaching Belleville with watchful eyes.

We lean on the bars of the Metro, watching and waiting. A sparkling tingle of anticipation hangs in the air, not a gendarme in sight for the first time in a long time. The streets hum with the quiet business of a winter's evening in the banlieue, Chinese supermarkets bustling next door to Turkish shops, well-heeled Parisians shuffling between them smoking Gauloises, old men with chic moustaches and young ladies, their hair covered with headscarves.

We wait and watch.

Then, we hear them.

Coming up from the underground, the boom-boom-clack of bass and snare, followed by the sharp rattle and a blast of whistle, growing louder and stronger, emerging from the Metro entrance out into the streets to be greeted with ragged cheers and an appreciative laugh of release. It is the samba band from Rhythms of Resistance, 30-plus strong, decked in pinks and floral tributes, emerging into the evening air.

Boom boom clak! Ba-boom-ba-boom clak-clak!

Bodies crowd around them, maybe 200 strong, faces from the march and strangers too, some already masked and punching the air, the cries of "*Anti-capitalista*!" stronger and fiercer than ever, ringing through the streets in time to the band. Soon they have taken the road, and traffic must wait, backing up bemused and patient behind them. Our brick nods to each other, and we step into the road, becoming part of the mass, and *them* becomes *us*.

Boom-clack ba-boom-ba-boom clak!

We turn, as one, down a side-street, following the samba band and whoever might be at the head of this march. On the pavements we see older persons, shopkeepers, people with bags of cheese and baguettes, clutching a child's hand whilst raising a supportive fist to salute us. People are smiling, happy to see the wild and the free marching in defiance of fear and oppression. All the while the cries ring from the buildings, my throat hoarse: *"ah-ha! Anti! Anti-capitalista-ha! Anti! Anti-capitalista!"*

Boom-clak! Ba-boom-boom-clak!

The moment is long, the energy increases, so do the number of masks, the feeling of imminent explosion. I am reminded of the Fuck Parades in London, of the Long Week in Rigaerstrasse, the anti-ISA protests in Kuala Lumpur, the liminal moments when parties evolve into riots. The lessons of the legal warning occasionally ring in my memory, but more than anything, I savour this sensation of collective liberation.

Boom! Boom! Boom! Clak-clak-clak!

Blue lights strobe the darkening sky with ultramarine. The urgency of the march picks up, confused commands and bursts of running down the streets. Blue lights ahead, and blue lights behind – the kettle is closing in. We find an alleyway to the right, and soon 200 people are streaming down it, people dragging their drums along and dumping over bins and trollies into the streets behind them. Someone falls, tripping another over them as they crash to the ground, others stopping to pull them up and encourage them onwards. Energy is bordering on panic now.

We emerge breathless on the far side, next to the canal. Dozens of people are still filtering through behind us and it seems that we have evaded capture – for the moment.

We spot the blue lights assembling at the road bridge, 200 metres up from us. People are calling to hurry – *"Allez! Allez!"* – and we move instinctively away from the lights.

Ahead, there is a narrow footbridge over the canal, and beyond that yet more police cars. The noose is closing.

People begin to run, seeing the opportunity to escape slipping away. The bridge rattles and clatters as people pound over it.

In the rush, I lose the others. I stop on the far side of the canal looking for them. People race past.

The sting of pepper spray on the wind hits me, searing my nostrils and eyes. The police have trapped perhaps 50 people on the opposite side of the canal – just where we were. Even from 20 metres away it is a raw and spicy wind. I am already moving, heart pounding in my chest, attempting innocence and anonymity, suddenly alone and vulnerable, unsure of who or what is awaiting on this side, or what will happen to those trapped behind.

I begin walking, pulling my mask off, heading up the canal where there seems to be space between the police. People sit eating baguettes and drinking wine on benches, watching the spectacle of a mass of black-clad people trapped between two lines of stormtroopers. I am calling my brick, hearing garbled messages from them. They have got across.

* * *

Later that evening, we are outside la Generale – the huge warehouse space the local squatters keep on lock-and-key for when they need a performance space. Inside is rammed to the rafters with smiling, laughing, leaping, euphoric crowds of people, leaping and stomping as the famous brass band from the march hammers through a borderline violent version of *Bella Ciao*. Every song they have played, every refrain, for the last hour, and even in the pauses between, the cry can be heard like a war chant:

"Ah-ha! Anti! Anti-capitalist a-ha! Anti! Anti-capitalist!"

We are drunk and exhausted, our eyes still stinging from the pepper spray, greeting survivors from the kettle on the canal as they drift back, grinning with giddy relief.

"They kept us there maybe an hour. I had a backpack full of equipment. I had to throw it into the canal. But still, after one hour, they let us all go. No arrests."

"I guess they know it's over."

"For now."

We are drinking cans of Maximator – 11 per cent strength beer that sizzles like gasoline in our stomachs and fires up our exhilarated chatter.

"So we did it. Somehow we did it. Sixty people on the streets ready to stand between the cops and 20,000 protesters like some kind of weird human condom."

"It could have been so different. I'm bloody relieved that nothing happened," Oak is saying. "That talk they gave us about raising our hands up with our fingers bent so the truncheons didn't break them. I was, like, God, what have we gotten into?"

"Yeah. I guess it was all fine. But was it enough? I mean, I have friends at home who would be horrified to know I was part of a 'de-escalation team'. They are the guys who believe that nonviolence protects the state, and that if we really wanted change, we have to fight for it on the streets."

"But if you have a riot, you won't have all these families and this creative atmosphere."

"Maybe it would have been different, but also they would have just demonised the whole thing as being about 'left-wing extremists hijacking the peaceful march'. The same old narrative. My biggest worry is how complicit we have become in working with the cops, the politicians, the whole status quo."

"It'll all ripple out, George. It'll all ripple out somehow."

We smile, then laugh a little more as the brass band chunters inside and the anti-capitalists *a-ha!* away. Through the windows, I can see faces beaming with delirious exhaustion, dancing away with stomping feet and fists pumping the air, and I am relieved it isn't all broken heads and handcuffs and eyes red raw from tear gas. I suck at the Maximator, retch at how flat it is, and suddenly feel my legs wobble.

"Shall we?"

We round up our little crew and head off into the Parisian night. Flashing blue lights illuminate the boulevards, casting sapphire shadows against the tall trees and art deco facades of the buildings.

As we pass the orange-and-yellow frontage of a McDonald's, Oak suddenly squeals and runs ahead, laughing but flustered.

"There was a guy! There was a guy wanking in the McDonald's!"

I can't help but look, and there indeed sat at the little shelf-bar in the window are two kettle-faced men, leering at us as we pass. One has his tracksuit pants open, and is pulling with frenzied focus at an unimpressive lump of meat under the table top. He is staring straight out, and for a moment I wonder if he is looking at us, or his own reflection.

I smile at him, hawk a huge ball of phlegm out of my throat, and spit it at the window. It splatters satisfyingly right at his eye level and slides down, a green nugget of sap and gristle. He pauses, looking shocked, and I flip him a rigid middle finger, before darting off down the street after the others.

"Ladies and gentlemen, the lackeys of capitalism," I sneer. "They're all fucking perverts."

4

The Shit Colony

This is what you should do: Go to your record store and buy all the KRÜ KRU recordings you can find. If they don't have any in stock, tell them to order some. If they refuse, then do what you have to do. Call radio stations and demand. Spray paint "KRÜ KRU" everywhere. Make them aware that the disease and the Scumfuc tradition is still spreading. Write "KRÜ KRU" on all your dollar bills. Any bills you have. People do not throw money away, so it would be a free way to get the message out. You must do it every day of your life. We must live for the Rock 'N' Roll underground. It CAN be dark and dangerous again. It CAN be threatening to our society as it was meant to be. IT MUST BE UNCOMPROMISING. And with me as your leader, it will happen. I am ready to lead you, my allies, into the real Rock 'N' Roll underground. Let's get started.

Adapted from GG Allin's Mission Statement

The mattress fell from the third floor of the Shitness like a drunken Tetris block, ricocheting clumsily off the pink A painted into the pavement outside the front door. I stood laughing with the trolley laden with crap, looking up as Mierda put the finishing touches to the graffiti in each window of each floor. Overall, it spelt out the marvellous edict – "HOMELESSNESS IS COOL WIPE YER BUM WITH THE NEWS" in shocking pink.

It felt good to be moving, like rats paddling in the toilet bowl. We were moving less than 250 metres, past the derelict shell of Non Commerical House, a free shop I first visited back in 2009 with Noodles, and around the corner to nothing less than the Colony itself, spitting distance from Shoreditch High Street Station and the hulking warehouses of Squatopolis Now, with fine views of the forest that had retaken the old redbrick railway flyover.

While the others redecorated the inside of the Shitness with appropriate messages for the bailiffs, myself, Fyodor and Awi took a long, long ladder and strolled down the road. As the sun rose, we propped it above the door and scrambled up through a tiny hatch to the inside. It looked the same as it had six months before on the abortive first attempt to open, and together we passed a morning angle-grinding the locks off from the inside. It rained steadily, a typical bank holiday Monday at the end of summer, no doubt dousing the carnival over in Notting Hill. We watch querulously when a pack of lycra-clad hipsters arrive at the bridge opposite and commence to pogo and bounce in unison on matching sets of kangaroo-shoes.

"Fucking hipsters," says Awi, over the squeal and sparks of the angle grinder.

"What?" shouts Fyodor over the racket.

"I said, FUCKING HIPSTERS!"

Mierda delivers some glutinous Chinese food after a few hours which we tie to the end of a rope and pull up through the same hatch we had entered. Across from us, a 24-hour car wash is servicing Beamers and Mercedes whilst we stand in the windows and scoop greasy chow mein into our mouths with hands covered in dust.

By evening, the door is open and new bolts are secured. The toilet there flushes, what unbelieveable luxury, and with mattresses arriving from the Shitness, we will have something to sleep on amidst the tomblike dust.

We gather for breakfast, croissants from the bins, Polish beer from the shop. Frank Zappa begins to drift from Mierda's room, and I recognise with amused delight the rapacious disco rattle of *Po-jama People* begin to rattle through the arches and hallways. Sunlight streams through the tall windows on to the little corner we have turned into a slum of cushions and food. Nieszka puts a pair of black stilettos on to her hands and sidles around the big room like a demented crab person. Lice is smoking and slurping tea from a mug branded with a bulldog's drooling maw. Grizzly is padding around with a busted football, looking expectantly from one to the other in hopeful earnestness.

"This is the fourth fucking time, man. Fucking Shitford House, I can't believe it. The first time we were here it lasted like four months, the next year two. Now it will probably be a fucking IPO. There's still all Bezdalius' drawings all over the walls at the back."

We tour around examining them, Mierda rediscovering them like hieroglyphs of her past. Bezdalius' line drawings are of mutant police with pig snouts and rotten phalluses spilling from their ragged uniforms, faces all twisted in forms of bestial brutality. Mierda's room, the same as each time she had returned, bears the single epitaph: *All Cocks Are Created Equal, But Some Are More Often Erected Than Others.*

From the far end of the building, electric with erotic agony, comes the sounds of Bill and Pinky either fucking or slowly torturing each other to death. Possibly both. They had arrived at 3am, sheepishly at the door, reporting that the bailiffs had turned up and unceremoniously interrupted their party and kicked them out.

"We left our vibrating egg there," explained Pinky.

"It was covered in shit anyway," smirked Bill. And off they'd gone to find a room of their own.

Mierda turns Frank Zappa up louder.

"They've been in here since the last time. They cleared out all the shit from the basement," says Nieszka, click-click-clicking around the floorboards. "It was fucking disgusting, like a muffin top. We barricaded it into one side of the room, but it's all cleared out now."

"Lucky for us," adds Lice. "Very considerate of them to

spruce the place up a bit."

"We did a party here once where we set a swing up in the bottom floor that you could only get to from a ladder. I spent nearly the whole night up there. I had diarrhoea. Everyone thought I was pissing." Mierda smiles at the memory.

"We lived downstairs and these fucking hipster cunts lived on the upper floor, and we found out after a few months that they'd been putting this place on Secret London or some shit and charging people 16 quid to come round and party and experience 'hidden London'. I spent weeks collecting shit from everyone to make it into poop icing to put on cupcakes and serve at one of their fucking parties, but we got evicted before we could do it."

"Didn't you film some movie here?"

"Oh yeah, *Illuminati Squatters vs Religious Zombies*. What ever happened to that?"

Mierda moans and rolls her eyes as Awi appears dutifully with his laptop and is scouring YouTube. We gather around the screen with our teas and roll-ups as Mierda disappears and Awi whoops excitedly when he finds it. It's a ten-minute teaser, featuring the very room we were sitting in, and outside shots of the bridge and the road.

Bezdalius is the main character, a weird street punk with an eyepatch and green and black spiked hair like a demented hybrid of man and palm tree. In the film, a shitcore experiment in zombie tribute, he steals some suitcase containing mystery juice that infects a bunch of religious zombies, who the squatters then fight and kill in pseudo-Matrix style on the streets outside. Mierda runs around screaming a lot in it, looking fresh and clean. There's lots of fake blood, and simulated masturbation, and fantastic costumes. It looks like a lot of fun.

Mierda returned with a coffee. "Is it over yet?"

"You look so young!" laughs Awi.

"Fuck off."

"What happened to the finished film?"

"I don't know. Nothing more ever came of it. I was drinking a lot of whisky at the time. It was fun though. Bezdalius used to be good for that kind of thing. He was never just sitting around, doing nothing. He always had some project. Not like now. What the fuck am I doing with myself? My time?

"We did a Litter Shitter here as well. It was before we sorted through all the trash bags to see if there was anything sharp in them. Me, Bezdalius and Fyodor had made these giant fucking cop uniforms and beat the living shit out of each other, throwing poop at everyone and Bezdalius dragging this massive crucifix through the carnage. Fyodor got a cut on his hand like six inches long. After that we made sure to look through the bags."

"Litter Shitter. What was that?"

"It was our performance. Bezdalius made the sound, like harsh noise shit, and we'd make these costumes and bring in tons of trash and just fight each other in it. Sasha or someone would do the Djing. We did it all over, until people figured out what it was, and then we had to start looking for gigs overseas. A few places here were really upset at what we did to their places. It was fun. Part of Bezdalius' GG Allin trip. It was good to get the anger out. What the fuck do we do nowadays?"

"Well. That's why we are going to France right? To make some money and get the fuck out of London for a while," said Nieszka.

"When? This is the first I've heard of it," I ask.

"It's girls only," says Nieszka.

"Yeah, no cocks allowed," laughs Mierda with her deep throaty chuckle.

"That's sexist," says Awi.

"Who's going?"

"Me, Naiad, Lice, Nieszka. It's three weeks picking grapes in some place in France with unlimited booze and food. It's supposed to be amazing. I just need to get out of this fucking country for a while, man."

"Yeah, me too." I feel a little excluded, especially after we had all been so close this last month, but what could I say? There are no expectations, no obligations, we are just washed together and making as good as we could.

"Fine. Screw you guys. I'll just stay here alone," pouts Awi.

"Yeah alone, with Pinky and Bill and Raitus and all your hipster sluts skipped off the streets of Shoreditch."

"Actually, that's a good point. When you all leaving?"

I first met Mantha at the Well Furnished squat in Hackney back in that disastrous, torturous, sublime summer of 201x. We had had an open-door policy for the first month, when we were still idealistic and the insanity of such a concept hadn't quite sunk in. I had signed up to be on the front desk, and after dutifully dragging myself from the leather sofa I called a bed, had run up the shutters and cracked the front door to look out on a sun-soaked yard in front of the Tesco's. I had barely plonked my feet up on to the desk when a long lean creature swung through the front door like a waltzing tiger and slipped into the chair in front of me.

"So, what's this squatting thing all about then?"

We spent the next hour pleasantly chatting and running through the basics of occupying and maintaining, legalities and difficulties, benefits and drawbacks. It was smooth and easy, and very quickly a rapport was built. So much so, that afterwards I offered to take her out around the area and point out a few of the local empties.

I had unwittingly unleashed a demon.

Mantha took to squatting like a simile takes to a sentence.

She tore through Hackney with a crowbar and a cheeky grin, becoming famous for often having two or more properties open in the area that she cycled between. Holiday homes, she called them. She brought others in, showing them the ropes and setting them off on their own autonomous adventures.

So when we heard that there was a lone squatter besieged in a yard in Jubilee Street, Whitechapel, penned in by security and refusing to come out, it came as no surprise that it was her.

The siege tactic is often used by the council, companies or organisations with enough capital behind them to essentially starve out the occupants of a squat, using the necessity of occupation against those inside. Hi-viz clad security agents will be placed at all entrances and exits, and those inside in legal occupation of the property will be calmly and clearly informed that they will be allowed out, but no one else shall be allowed in.

And so begins the battle of wills.

Jubilee Street is a yard and set of offices owned by the council of Tower Hamlets. It'd been squatted previously, already evicted and guardians installed in the offices. However, the high-walled yard still contained a number of little rooms, a trailer and a small forest, that had apparently appealed to Mantha and some friends.

When security arrived and informed her of the conditions of the Siege, Mantha was alone inside, and after listening carefully, informed the guards that she wished them the best of luck, before going back to bed.

We pop around on the first, second and third day to check on her, taking requests for supplies, speaking to her through the metal door and throwing bags of food and weed over the high wall to her when the guards aren't looking. This was already longer than any squat had held out to a siege, as far as we knew, and never with a solo occupant. Mantha was nonplussed. She spends her time sleeping, chilling out and, in fact, thoroughly enjoying her isolation.

By the night of day four, we decide to escalate the situation.

Awi, Mierda and me are drunk when we arrive at Jubilee Street, having strolled down from the Shit Colony with Grizzly padding happily beside. When we arrive, another group who have been hanging out pestering the guards is there.

"Ah, the next shift! Ready to take over then?" smiles one of them.

Dutifully, after saying a quick hello to Mantha, we quickly turn to the much more stimulating task of haranguing the security over concepts of guard culture and class solidarity, alternating between stinging wit and jocularity to apoplectic indignation and hostility, never expecting them to suddenly cast off their jacket and join us, but experiencing these moments as the cutting edge of refining our beliefs, as with cops, bailiffs, judges and others who would stand with the Quo. Typically, they frame their responses as justifications essentially summarised as "If I don't do it, someone else will" and "Because that's what is normal".

Not being tyrants, we also allow space for such people to ask questions. Without fail, the questions form around the following themes:

"Why don't you pay rent like normal people?"

"Why don't you get a job like normal people?"

"What gives you the right to squat in someone else's property?"

"Why don't you have a wash?"

And we also have our preferred modes of questioning.

"Who's the boss here? I want to speak to the top man."

"Can I ask you? How much do they pay you for this? So, if I offer you more money, does that mean you'll work for me and do what I say?"

"What if I am an undercover millionaire? What then? If I produce the readies will you drop working for the council and come work for me? Or you have some sort of chauvinist loyalty to Tower Hamlets?"

"Do you know what a mercenary is?"

"Why are you holding this person prisoner?"

"Do you feel bad about being a class traitor, or do you just not feel?"

"How do you sleep at night?"

"If she starves to death in there, would you consider that a victory? Would you feel responsible?"

"Release the hostage!"

"Why don't you join us? You can come live in the squat with us!"

"It's great, free rent, good times, smelly a bit but you get used to that."

"Bring the kids! And the wife!"

Whilst this is going on, one or two of us keep breaking off and quickly run around the walls to look for possible entry points. It is growing darker, and pairs of people are hanging around, chatting to Mantha through the gate or drinking in the car park. The three security guards are relaxing, distracted by the derisive questioning and enjoying some class banter.

"You see, why you protecting the rich man's property? Why you defending the state against your fellow man? You think the rich care if you get socialised health, or get treated fair by employers and banks? Why you imprisoning this person? Why don't you join us? We'd take care of you. We all look after each other. We make sure no one is ever homeless. No one of us is ever out on the streets. Look at you. Where's your boss now? Where the big man at? They aren't here. They don't care. You think our genderfluid friend in there ever going to get tired? They at home. They's chilling. They good to go whilst we creating your job. Without us, you don't have no work. We generating this economy."

Whilst this goes on, I run to the other side. There is a metal fork jutting from the corner of the wall. I try to pull myself up, drunkenly levering myself halfway up the wall before the greasepaint the metal is smeared in warps my grip and I drop exhausted and impotent back to the pavement.

When I return to the other side, Awi is loading a makeshift

ladder of blue rope out of a bag and checking the knots. Everything happens at once. The hi-viz security guards suddenly rush us. Awi and Mierda are shouting. The ladder is halfway over the wall. One guard charges into us and I put my hands up to collect him. Somehow my hands wipe greasepaint over the immaculate garish yellow of his jacket. The guy shrieks in disgust, turning and retreating. Grizzly is barking incessantly. Everyone is yelling.

Then Mierda is gone, Grizzly too. The guards are all shouting and complaining, their authority challenged, they are on the phone to the police. Me and Awi collect the ladder and decide to withdraw.

We were on Bethnal Green Road sometime later, drunkenly rambling and swaggering about the pavement, bloated on our mischief.

"We should get that scaffold from the library man, can you imagine? Proper siege tower style. Loads of crusties hanging off the top with grappling hooks and flaming torches. Just roll it right down Jubilee Street at midnight and slam it against the wall, pile them over the top and in before they know what's hit them."

"It'd be appropriate. It was right around here on Sidney Street that two Latvian anarchists held off against the police and the military around 1900, back when the whole East End was riddled with Russian emigres and *messugannah* politicos, dealing with things with the pistol and the knife, according to the press. As sympathetic then as now."

"Things change so little really."

"There was even an anarchist club right on Jubilee Street."

"There is now."

We laugh, and head to a chicken shop where I wash the greasepaint from my hands and then cover them with chicken grease again. Awi continues to wax.

"The Siege of Jubilee Street. A century ago it was guns and Latvian bank robbers. Now it's one stoner refusing to come out and the council penning them 's been a hundred years of policing by consent and compromise by the working classes since then. Greatest PR campaign in history. Now we're all so fucking well behaved."

"You see them change when there's a sniff of violence. It's all nicey-nicey chat and diplomacy until the first bottle thrown then *bam*, down comes the hammer and the baton."

"We're living with the ghost of history, Awi. It's screaming in our fucking ear."

"Fuck it, let's go back to Shoreditch and see what's happening on the street. Maybe we can pick up some Spanish girls and have a fourgy."

"OK."

We head out the chicken shop chuckling, heading back down the Bethnal Green Road towards Shoreditch when the police car rolls up and two cops jump out. One of them has jowls like two balls of fat left out for the sparrows, the other a face like a blank piece of paper.

Jowls fingers me immediately.

"You. You're under arrest."

"What? What for?"

"Common assault. You've been identified."

"As what?"

"White man with dreadlocks wearing camouflage."

"That could describe almost anyone in Shoreditch, come on."

Too late. They read me the rights and Paperface slaps the cuffs on me as I stand mutely protesting my innocence in numb disbelief. Awi looks stunned, for once lost for words, as they load me into the back of the van, his mouth open in a frozen moment of indecision. It was like being kidnapped off the street. My whole evening changed very quickly.

In the back of the van, I realise they had forgotten to take my phone off me. I manage to wriggle it out, and text to Mierda, letting her know that I've been arrested. Not that it matters. It was going to be a long evening.

They leave me the book I have in my pocket. Something by Aldous Huxley. Not the famous one. It seems incongruous to be reading about the upper classes hoi-polloing about their summer home from within the confines of the cell. They keep checking in on me over the night. I refuse the food. It's like cardboard tapioca. In the morning, a policeman with the build of a garden shed, who uncannily resembled Tosh from *The Bill*, pulls me out of the cell, feigning neutrality.

"I don't know what happened, I'm just here to find out," he was saying as he led me to the interview room.

"I don't know either. I was just getting some chicken with my mate. It's funny, he's the black one, it's normally him who gets nicked for no reason."

"Well I don't know about that. Apparently there was some incident. I'm just here to get to the bottom of it. If that guy charged you then it's self-defence isn't it?"

"Yes. Self-defence. He came running right at me. Madness. And there they are imprisoning that poor guy in there. Hired thugs I tell you."

"Well that's right. Let's just get it all sorted out shall we."

Into the room we go, chatting back and forth quite amicably, as if my imprisonment were nothing more than a delay in awaiting the butler to bring my coat so I might go out on to the tennis lawns that afternoon at the summer house. It's all rather relaxed and jolly. I had been rather bored as fuck waiting in that room and was enjoying the opportunity to hear my own voice.

He sits me down in the comforting sterility of the interview room and runs me through how it's going to work.

"Interview number SHMEE-SHMA-SHMOO commencing at ten thirty-three on morning of September 17th 201x, with Police

Sergeant Tosh. So, Mr F., can you confirm that you were present at Jubilee Street on the evening of the sixteenth at around 10pm?"

"No comment."

His face drops like a souffle from the oven once he realises what was going to happen during the next 20 minutes. I drink his disappointment with relish.

"Can you explain in your own words what happened that night?"

"No comment."

"Can you tell me who the other people there with you were?"

"No comment."

"We understand that there was a dog there as well. Can you tell me who that belonged to?"

"No comment."

"There was an accusation that one of the security guards there was assaulted? Did one of them try to assault you?

"No comment."

"You realise that if they attacked you first and you defended yourself that that is self-defence?"

"No comment."

"You understand what self-defence is?"

"No comment."

It goes on in this manner for a while, with Tosh trying to angle it one way or another. Long hours waiting in a cell have allowed me time to wonder and imagine how officers prepare themselves for these interviews, consulting with superiors and sergeants and reviewing Interrogation for Dummies, selecting which particular psychological template to utilise in order to approach their victim. I had spotted the selection of chummy neutrality as soon as he had opened the door and invited us out, so relaxed and natural, as if we were off for Pimm's by the poolside.

At the end, he switches it off.

"Well, I think you've done yourself a disservice there,

George."

"Well, I'd like to do a disservice to the guy who shopped me. And that's Mr F. to you."

I shouldn't have spoken. They release me on bail, with the condition not to return to Jubilee Street, and six weeks until I would receive notice of further action. I am to return to Bethnal Green Police Station on October 18th – the day of the Anarchist Bookfair.

On the way out, I am signing out my possessions, and the desk sergeant looks at my hand tattoo.

"What does ACAB mean?" he asked.

"All cops are beautiful."

He blanches.

I smile, and skip out, to nobody waiting, nobody caring. I have no idea where I am, somewhere east and forlorn, no idea which direction to go. I have lost 17 hours of my life, arbitrarily punished no matter what the outcome of their investigations, now marked and listed for at least the next six weeks. I spit in disgust at no one in particular, and turn to walk the long way back through a grey miserable east London to an uncaring squat.

Mantha held out for 12 days, before the council gave up, and let them have the squat. We reckon she could have done a month easily.

Barnabas is complaining. He's earned his right to complain. He's been at Claremont Road during the M11 road protests, when the cops had torn hundreds of protesters from the scaffold towers erected on the roofs of buildings marked for demolition for the new roads. He's got face tattoos. He's obviously done enough acid to perplex and bewilder the entire district of Haight-Ashbury for a day. He likes cake and ice cream now, and often would be found frying a solo steak in the kitchen. He'd once asked us all totally upfront if we were all 'into this class war thing, then'. One of his eyes permanently looks the other way. He smiles like a cheeky schoolboy, and dutifully drives us to parties in the back of his van as he doesn't drink much any more. Once, he told me that he needed to practise speaking more, as sometimes he could lapse into silence like a monk. He set himself a word count, but I never knew how he kept track.

He rocks back up after an absence of months. The Shitness had been beneath his standards, but now we were in the Colony he could find himself a spot to occupy with his delightful if simple dog Flower, who flopped around him like a sack of puppies that had learned enough coordination to scavenge food and shit everywhere it could.

"There's no air in here, man, I can't breathe. How can we open a window?"

"Well, just smash a small one," I say. After all, I'd broken a window on the Shit Colony two years before. It seemed appropriate.

"You think? Will that be alright?"

This is what happens when the reckless and the feckless make plans together.

We decide that I will go down on to the street and keep an eye out, whilst he smashes the window, to ventilate the space.

Dutifully, I shuffle out the main door and stand opposite the Colony, beer in hand, whilst Barnabas peers out from the upstairs window.

I look around, and give him the nod.

With a huge booted kick he blasts out one of the panels, and glass rains down on to the pavement. I am already heading back in, when I hear an irate and furious cry.

"OI!"

It is a man with the build and demeanour of a steroid-addicted bulldog.

"You can't fucking do that! You fucking can't do that!"

He is sidling along the road, screaming up at the confused figure of Barnabas in the now open window pane. His eyes pop in his skull and veins in his neck. He is apoplectically incensed over what he has witnessed.

"Come down here now! Come down here! You had better clean this shit up right now! What if people have dogs?"

I realise how much I did not want to deal with this shit. Why have I got involved at all in this scheme? I hadn't suffered from a lack of air, I hadn't wanted an open window, all I had done was try to help, and now this.

Barnabas comes down, looking fierce. I move next to the door of the Colony.

The Bulldog keeps shouting and shouting.

"You can't just smash a window like that."

"I'm going to clean it up, get out of my face."

Somehow, it escalates so quickly I cannot follow. Bulldog slaps Barnabas across one tattooed cheek, and Barnabas swings a massive booted foot up at him. There is a scuffle, t-shirts pulled and pushes and curses, but it quickly calms down again.

There is a second man, a quiet skinhead who has appeared from nowhere, and together him and Barnabas sweep up broken glass and collect it. So far, everything seems fair, and I watch from the doorway of the Colony, a beer in hand.

Barnabas comes inside. I stay in the doorway.

"Barnabas, get the fuck upstairs, stop provoking them."

Then the Bulldog is in front of me.

"Come on then, get your whole crew down. We'll take them all on."

I see the St George flag sewn on the sleeve of his jacket. The quiet one is eyeballing me.

"Look, we cleaned it up from the street. It's over now. Let's leave it."

Bulldog continues, in a hiss, squaring up to me:

"What if we want to come inside? Who's going to stop us?"

"You are not crossing this fucking doorway. Just fuck off."

Opening my mouth turned out to be just what they were

waiting for.

Suddenly the Quiet One gave a monstrous roar, powering himself up with an arced spread of his limbs and bellowing:

"Fucking Lefty!"

He smashes the beer can out of my hand and down on to the floor. He swings and I catch it square on my upper lip, tottering backwards my head swimming, feeling the back of my skull slam against the bannister of the stairs.

Stunned moments, unable to move, senses reeling and misfiring as I lay on the concrete steps wondering if I would ever stand again. Somehow, I am aware of the door slamming shut, the lock going on, people shouting.

I propel myself up, adrenaline surging, and then feel hot blood fill my mouth and jet from the hole punched in my face. I stagger about, trying to catch the fluid splashing from my face, and on automatic my legs carry me up the stairs to the toilet to tear off some tissue to plug against it. Front and back, face and bone, I feel like I've been skull-fucked.

I can push the tip of my tongue through a slit between my septum and top lip.

Awi is already on his phone.

"You're going to need stitches. Here, the Royal Hospital is nearest, but this is the best option for facial cosmetic surgery, they have a better record."

"How the fuck do you know this? I'm just going to the nearest one. Fucking hell, where is everybody? Is anybody else in?"

"It's ok. They've gone. I can walk with you to the hospital."

"For fuck's sake. No, it's fine, I'll go. Just fucking stay here in case they come back."

As Awi opens the door for me, Mierda and Naiad are pulling up on their bikes.

"What happened?"

"Fucking fash, fucking Barnabas, fucking bullshit. I'm off to the fucking hospital to get my fucking face sewn up. I've got a fucking hole in my face."

Mierda looks at me. "Yeah. You should get that sewn up. I've got a tattoo to do."

"Fine."

I fuck off to get three stitches in my face. I'll be left with a lightning bolt scar on my lip as a memento, some fucked up Harry Potter tribute.

I return four hours later, my lip now swollen like a buttock, and find Barnabas skulking around, boz-eyes spinning in guilty directions.

"Well, what can I say?"

I look at him. He smiles with the startling innocence of an acid-fed hound.

"They came back. Said they wanted that to be the end of it. No police involved. No reprisals."

"Great. How's your room? Plenty of air now?"

"Oh yeah, it's great."

"Brilliant."

5

The Blank Earth

There are no passengers on spaceship Earth: we are all crew.
Marshall McLuhan

Tearing through the pitch-black night, the road begins to weave drunkenly from side to side, the autostop robo-petrol dispensers and sparse towns now given way to only claustrophobic hedgerows and tightly packed forests of shadowy trees. The headlights pick out creature after creature flinging itself across the road impetuously: stout white-masked badgers, tiny shuffling bundles of hedgehogs, a long and lean martin, scurrying out in front of us, eyes suddenly glowing diamonds in the glare of the headlights.

The road climbs upwards, ever upwards, coiling through the mountains with only the steady rumble of the engine and the ceaseless beat of techno as we ascend towards Lice and Nico's place.

Soon, the road is almost too steep and too narrow, we daren't go further, having been warned to park further down the hill and await further instructions. We don't care, we leap out with our bottle of almond liquor and stretch our legs, slowly beginning the climb upwards into the dark. The road sluices one way, and we peer at signs and try to listen to the sound of a party, or music, or voices, or anything, but all around is only the deafening silence of the woods at night.

"Just be careful here, ok," I say paternally. "This isn't the kind of place they call the police if they think you are a burglar. This is the kind of place they just shoot you."

The road forks off in different directions, each direction marked by the name of the family that lives there. None of us can remember Nico's surname, or even if we have ever heard it. Someone makes an educated guess, and we push further up the hill.

We can see lights on up ahead – a small hamlet of stone buildings, whitewashed with red tile roofs. To the left, the low angled slant of a cow-shed, now lit up from the inside with fairy lights. Beyond, we can see the outline of a sheltered food space, and the murmuring laughter of giggling voices.

We stroll right in, discovering a trio of surly men drinking pastis and wobbling from side to side, grinning inanely at one another.

We stand, a little uncertainly, and they carry on their conversations before suddenly starting and looking at us with saucer eyes.

I launch into my GCSE French – I know how to win friends in France.

"Bonjour, mes amis! La maison de la Nico et Lice, c'est ici? Nous avons les copains de la Lice. Tu comprends, la'Lice? Ca va?"

The French are delighted and raise cheerful glasses and bottles of beer, chattering at us at a relentless pace. My French makes it less than three sentences further in:

"S'il vous plait, tu parler beaucoup rapidement! Moins rapide, s'il vous plait!"

"Ah! You are English? Alors, we 'ave to keep a count of how many there are of you!"

We all laugh. A second Frenchman seems surprised. "I have never heard him speak so much English!"

"Do you want some LSD?"

It becomes apparent that the three of them are tripping their balls off. I guess we have come to the right place. We open some beers thankfully, and pass around the almond liquor, and sink gratefully into the chairs around the table. They have constructed a long tent of wooden poles and tarpaulin down one side of the house, covering a lengthy dining table, an outdoor kitchen with hob and spices, and a little drinks section, where a couple of bottles of rum have helpfully been left out. We waste no time in investigating those, and settle for a few awkward moments to chat with the tripping Frenchmen, who introduce themselves as friends of Nico, from the grape-picking crew.

"How strong is this acid?"

"This one is only 250 mikes, it is normal. But I 'ave before 600."

"Wow. That's fort. Tres fort."

He smiles, rolling his eyes in his head like sparkling marbles. One of the other men, with a leather jacket and a large pair of spectacles, stands next to me, his hand on my shoulders, giving me a gentle cuddle.

"It is good to be close together," he says, in a rolling French accent.

Naiad and Mierda look overwhelmed, and after a few more moments of rolling, chattering, broken French and laughter, we make our excuses and retreat back around the corner, promising to see them all in the morning, for "pastis pour le petit dejeuner", which amuses them to no end.

As we round the corner, we find Wierzbowski hovering around, holding a tiny, brown and white puppy.

"Wierzbo! You're here!"

We all hug and halloo and coo over the puppy.

"I skipped a dog," he is saying. "Can you believe it? I get fucking pissed off one day and go for a walk, and this little thing just comes wandering out of the woods towards me. I can't believe it. He doesn't have microchip, no one in the village knows where he came from, no collar. I don't know what I'm going to do man."

"Unbelievable! You come all this way and you manage to skip a dog."

We laugh, happy to be reunited, even though it has only been a month, it feels like so much longer. We sit up for a while longer, drinking rum and beer and the almond liquor, before exhaustion finally overtakes us, and we limp down the hill to pull the van closer to the house and steal a few hours sleep before the sun comes up.

In the morning, Nico and Lice give me the tour around their land – a long slant of hillside rolling down towards the cow-shed they have lovingly restored and converted into a remarkable little home. They have an orchard of apple, plum and cherry, with huge old pear trees growing at the top, and an area to one side cleared and terraced into a vegetable patch growing beans, potatoes, courgettes and pumpkins. At the top, a compost toilet has been installed, and off to one side, a large disused barn that still belongs to Nico's father, the stalls for the cows and the cages for the rabbits lying dusty and empty inside. The field beside it has a trio of vans and some cars already parked up, and we park the van a little further down the road, beside some trees for shade.

As the day warms, more and more people emerge from their tents and vans, and begin to rotate around the outdoor marquee they have erected, with beer and wine beginning to flow and an easy camaraderie settling over the group – an even split of weird UK-based punks and French seasonal workers. Daigas and Nieszka are there, with Mierda's long, sallow brother, our weird artist friend Nookie, fresh from the mental hospital, and her stag-like dog Medusa, Wierzbo and Valkata – a twin Gemini set of technopunks, dreadlocks and bright colours. Each worthy of a book about them, but not this one. The French are more uniformly neatly groomed, all grape-pickers of the *vandage*, but with the piratical garb that betrays their forest beggar nature: skull and cross-bone patches, flashes of gypsy fashion, occasional leather jackets. Together, we find a synthesis of understanding.

"When I first met Nico, I did not understand him," I am explaining to bright-eyed Timon, one of the workers, small and sparkle-eyed. "He came to London, but I think he really did not enjoy. We were staying in a terrible place, with no toilets, and we got evicted halfway through. But then we met him again for my birthday at Lice's mum's house in Devon, and we started to really get on. I think the neutral ground helped. Now, we have here a gathering of the tribes. The French freaks and the UK-Eastern Europe mob coming together for Lice's 30th. And to see them together is truly wonderful."

"Shall we all go for a swim before lunch?" suggests Lice, beaming in the doorway in obvious delight to see us all here. She left the UK nearly three years before – leaving for a three-week grape-picking adventure, and never coming back. We cheer in agreement.

We let gravity help us to trudge down the hillside, stumbling through the steep slopes of humus in our flip-flops. The air immediately cools as we enter the shade of the forest. We spot mushrooms erupting from the forest floor everywhere: bullet domes of silver, weird alien orange creatures with tentacles like starfish, bloated sacs of spores blooming next to dislodged caps of dirt they popped out with the force of their erection.

"Fungi. Fungi is the future," someone is murmuring. "We are all covered in fungi, all different kinds."

"Yeah I have cheesy-foot rot," says Mierda. "It's not much fun."

"Did you ever see *The Girl with All the Gifts*? Well, spoiler alert, that's about a parasitic, if not, symbiotic relationship forming between humans and some weird new fungi that arrives on Earth. The first thing it does is turn all the people who are bitten into transmitters for the disease, makes them just want to bite other people. But if you are pregnant when bitten, the child you give birth to is some kind of mutant hybrid of both. They still have that hunger to bite the uninfected, but they can control it to some degree, and they can learn. That's the key. They're still madly driven to spread the fungus, but they are capable of learning in a way that the adult infected cannot.

"So, in the end – spoiler alert – the dead infected start piling up on each other and these huge, fungal growths start bursting out of them. They basically grow into one huge giant mushroom tree thing, with millions of pods hanging from them. But the pods need fire in order to open, and then the spores become air born, basically infecting every last human on the planet, and therefore transforming them into nothing more than mushrooms, and then leaving the world to this new mutant generation of children who are half-fungus, half-human.

"It's about hope for humanity's survival through mutation in the face of environmental catastrophe. It's about the old versions of humanity needing to die off completely and be replaced by something that can live in harmony with nature."

We paddle in the river. Dragonflies dance around us, buzzing missile knives of jade and emerald sparkling in the sun, chasing one another. In the shallows formed by the slowing of the water, dozens of boatmen skate gently across the surface together in insect flotilla formation. The pack of dogs splashes in, and whilst the others lounge in the shade, we set about the serious work of beavering.

We were inspired by the shallowness of the swimming hole we were shown on the first day, and by examining the fallen trees that criss-crossed the river further down. They had caught the various branches and clods of leaves that were washing downstream, growing in thickness and sturdiness to a point where we questioned if in fact they had been built intentionally. When asked, Lice and Nico had shaken their heads.

"We should build dams!" I cry during one speed-fuelled Sunday afternoon. Me, Naiad and Mierda paddle naked in the sun, relentlessly pulling stones from the river bed and piling them across the waterways at selected locations to construct our own network of dams, living for a few hours as human-beaver mutants.

"The logic is sound," I explain as we pack smaller stones into the cracks in our constructions. "What causes flooding further downstream is too much water, moving too quickly. Chopping down all the trees, or making concrete runways, or draining swamps and marshlands means that the water flows much faster, collects much faster, builds up too fast and floods the place. Trees trap it and allow the ground to absorb it much better than grass or certainly concrete. But what we need is beavers. Beavers build dams, just like this, and they create pools upstream for the fish. Like where we want to swim, and downstream they create marshland. They help diversify the environment, and slow the flow of water. Look. Look at the water boatmen. They only like it where the current is less strong, but still moving. Now the dragonflies come to eat them. And then the birds will come to eat the dragonflies. And then the weasels will come to catch the birds. And so on.

"In some towns in Britain, this is how they are addressing the problem of flooding. With trees, and with beavers. Beavers man! They'll save us all! And fucking trees! Let's plant ten billion trees. How hard would that be? That's like 1.5 trees for everyone on the planet. That would sort some serious shit out in the world. And then beavers for the water problem."

The water here is mountain clear and fresh, running from a dozen streams in the area down into the crystal flowing waters of the river. After a few afternoons, we have constructed a series of dams, upstream from the fallen trees, that satisfyingly trap the water and raise it in places by up to 12 inches, allowing us to dunk ourselves over our heads and lie back, staring up at the elm and pine and ash trees that tower above it.

"Transpiration. The trees suck moisture out of the air. They suck it up from the ground too, but the most important thing they do is hold the soil together. They are all actually one organism, interconnected by mycorrhizae: a fungus that grows between the roots of all plants and organic matter."

"Just like in *The Girl With All The Gifts,*" laughs Lice.

"Exactly. In India, we considered ourselves 'soil farmers'. But that easily could have been 'fungus farmers'. We primarily worked to establish thick, healthy, living soil and then the fungus and nature took care of the rest. We built raised beds of sheet mulch, up to a metre high, layering logs and branches, soil and manure, topped off with pine needles, like lasagne sheets on top of each other, and bordering them with rocks. After a year, we pulled some of the stones aside, and inside was black, black, living soil. The whole place crawling with worms and ants and spiders and lizards and scorpions and all sorts. We never uprooted plants from the bed. In the first year, this weird little thing started to sprout in between all our beans and salad, and we just watched it, watched it explode, until someone finally identified it as a local type of almond tree that had taken root in our bed. We were thrilled. In the principles of agroforestry, this is the ideal: producing soil and environment closest to the qualities of a forest, with stacks of trees, shrubs, undergrowth, roots and vines, all tying it together on multiple levels."

"You're such a hippy," smirks Mierda, splashing around in the pool we have created.

"I don't think there's anything hippy about knowing my shit," I retort, sniffily. "I'm more of a soil nerd."

Pétanque is a version of boules, played with heavy metal balls, each carved with a different design to distinguish them. The objective is to land them as close as possible to the little "*cochonnet*" – the piglet – and to get to 13 points. If you have the two closest balls to the *cochonnet*, you get two points, if three, and so on. It is strangely satisfying, and during our stay at Les Souches, becomes our evening ritual, of beer and a couple of rounds between whoever is around.

We drink the little cheap beers, topping them up with orange liqueur, and smoke as we play.

"We will be fine up here when the climate change happens," Lice is saying as she prepares to throw his *pétanque* ball. "So the sea water level rises, but we are on top of the mountain. We have access to fresh water, we have the forest for wood. So the winters will get milder here or harder, but we won't be underwater. The storms might be worse, but we are still in a much better position than most people."

"You know how I describe it to people now?" I say. "I ask them: have you been to Miami? The Netherlands? How about Suffolk and Norfolk? The Maldives? Bangladesh? Well, go now. Go now, because in 20 years they'll all be underwater. They'll be gone."

"A piece of ice the size of Belgium just broke off from Antarctica and is now floating its way across the ocean. Just the size of Belgium. Just, snap, tralala, off it goes. All those penguins off on holiday," says Mierda.

"Off to Madagascar."

"Ugh! Madagascar. My brother was telling me, if you want to see it, go now. It's called 'last chance tourism'."

Clank! Go the *pétanque* balls, and excitedly we scurry over to measure how close they have landed to the cornichon. Smiles to the victors, some spirited grumbling amongst the losing team.

I turn to Timon. "Did you ever hear about the pirate colony on the north coast of Madagascar?"

"Ah, yes, yes. It was quite famous."

"Libertatia, they called it. Like a pirate utopia. Peoples from all over the world, all different nationalities, calling themselves 'the Liberi'. The 'enemies of slavery'. They were largely crews of mutineers, or freed slaves. They used to sail out on their ships and capture military vessels from other countries. When they caught them, they would ask the crews if their officers had been decent to them or not. If so, they let them elect if they should remain with them or not. If not, they put them on a little boat and cast them adrift. The crews could then choose whether to join the Liberi as free men, or if they wanted to take the ship and sail away. They were fucking cool man."

Clank! Wahey! Boo!

"I went to Madagascar one time. It is very close to my island, the Reunion Islands. So beautiful. So sad that it is being destroyed, but like everywhere I suppose. I feel like a pirate sometimes, cruising around in my little van. A land pirate," says Timon.

"Me too. With squatting in London, it's like guerrilla warfare. You're up against a much bigger, stronger enemy, one that would crush you in a direct confrontation. So what do you do? You hit-and-run. You strike where the capital is weak, get what you need, hold the position for as long as you can, but then instead of directly confronting, you pssst! Disappear back into the jungle. You find communities that will help you, other cells and units out there in the city, and you network and organise, surviving pending the big day when you are strong enough, or simply keeping the fire burning to pass on to another generation. Or at least, just to survive. They used to have a saying: 'when freedom is outlawed, only outlaws are free'. That's how it feels a lot of the time. Though technically, we aren't criminals. Though it feels like it."

"I only face the police one time in a squat in France," says Timon. "And I show them that ey, no, I am a worker. I show them my work cards. We all did. And they let us go."

"Me and Nieszka squatted an old abbotry when we were grape-picking in 2014. That place was lovely," says Lice. "No one ever came to bother us there."

Clank! Wahey! Boo!

"You know, there used to be two families that lived up here that absolutely hated each other." Nico lines himself up to take another throw. "Every day you hear them, shouting and screaming at one another. It was terrible. One woman and her son, and one old guy. For years, they would be screaming at each other, and the worst was they both had guns. It got so bad. One day, the old man, he shot and killed both of them. They threatened him before. Many times, and they went after him in the woods one day when he was hunting, and he just shot them both dead. He disappeared for a little while, then handed himself in to the police, and I guess now he is dead or in jail. It's pretty wild up here."

"Wilderness places," I say distantly. "In India where I lived was the same. The Valley of Death they called it. Two or three people used to disappear up there every year. It was the valley where they make *charas*. Used to be the major source for hashish until Morocco took over. You can go up there in the season and still find farmers teaching their children to hand roll the buds into super soft, super strong hashish that sells for like a euro a gram. All the smugglers and big dealers used to come. I imagine a lot still do."

We pour orange liqueur into our beers to top-up the strength, and Timon prepares slices of *sauscisson* to nibble on as we continue our game, chatting and smoking and laughing in the sunshine. It feels good to be free and out in the open, nothing more pressing than a routine of games and chattering and nonsense. Nothing more pressing than togetherness.

Clank! Wahey! Boo!

Maybe it's the heat. Maybe the pack mentality. Maybe Grizzly is just a fucking asshole.

I find Mierda back at the house, Lice kneeling before her, cleaning a savage gash across one leg. They had all left together, the two of them and five dogs, an hour before, and now she was back, covered in blood and tears.

"Grizzly just went for the others," she is saying, still shell-shocked. "Lice was holding Gina back, but Medusa and all the others were just going crazy. Grizzly locked on to Timon's dog, on to Maquis, and she wouldn't let go. I had to bite her. I had to bite her to get her to let go."

"There there," I say. "There there."

The sun is a disc of burning magnesium bleaching the cyan sky a sordid white. A lazy black twin-propellered bomber languidly arcs above us, droning and threateningly low, the shadow of a metal killer whale cruising like a predator seen as if from the bottom of a drying salt ocean. The tarmac blasts heat back up at us, and on either side fields of drooping sunflowers pay pious salutation to the midday heat, their amarillo crowns bowed in contemplative reverie.

The road to [location redacted] is not long, but in the midst of southern Europe's heatwave it seems like a flagellant pilgrimage as we scuff our flip-flops along baking tarmac between scant patches of shade.

Grizzly pauses to sniff quickly at the flattened and desiccated corpse of a rat, squashed flat in the gutter of the road. I pause to lean over it, admiring the glinting skeletal toes of feet that could not run fast enough, the warped and deformed head still tufted with bits of fur, the rest matted and baked to the texture of corkboard. Mierda quickly hurries Grizzly on. We bicker with the idle irritation of old friends caught too long between oases in the desert.

The first *supermarche* no longer exists it seems, so we continue our march through the idle French villages, bitterly feeling our skin cook and the moisture vape from our bodies. The gravel scratches our feet, so we jump an irrigation ditch and walk part of the way through arid grasses where giant leaf-green grasshoppers leap and dance as we pass. Grizzly makes a lazy attempt to jump after one, but it is too hot, especially for her with her shaggy sienna coat on.

After two more kilometres, we enter an area of wide car parks and concrete low-rises, grey and hissing in the heat. There, beyond the car park, the blue and yellow signage of our trans-

European economic oasis: the Didl.

Out the front, two smiling leprechauns, one with blue-green dreadlocks and the other with a charming fedora on, wave at us like cruise ship passengers greeting an arriving raft of castaways.

"It's Naiad and Timon," says Mierda, needlessly.

They had hitch-hiked down. Apparently the first car to pass had picked them up.

We trawl the carbon-copy rows of produce in the Didl, identical from London to Lisbon, Toulouse to Talinn, mapped out by shrewd and cynical marketeers so the order goes across Europe: cheap chocolate treats and biscuits, cute brotchen bread rolls in little stalls with local pastries thrown in for ethnic flavour, then the fruit and veg, gleaming and pristine in crates and boxes as if straight from the market. As you reach the back, you hit the dairy, and as ever we search in vain for the now seemingly discontinued vegan potato salad Mierda ate across Germany in years before. Loop around, ignoring the central rows of household products and the long, deep freezers of factory-slaughtered meat, as you begin to complete your circle you will find yourself at the booze shelves, pouring over wines and crates of beers, the spirit section here remarkably smaller than in other places, the addition of local delicacies of sweet white wines the name of which escapes me now.

"Fuck me," says Mierda. "Food is fucking expensive in France."

"No wonder there's riots throughout the year," I rumble.

Naiad and Timon practically skip through the aisles, giggling and laughing, as if in some food-themed amusement park.

Outside, in the oven, we sit on the pavement in a patch of shade and stare out at the rolling car park, burning white gravel under a burning white sky. The air shimmers, and Citroen cars roll back and forth, delivering plump and rose-cheeked French people in and out of the Didl. Shrivelled grandmothers wheel trollies into the store. We eat a simple picnic of beer, saucisson, baguette, fromage – our standard diet in France. I remark at how many identical car parks we must have sat in, outside how many identical Didls, all across Europe.

Then we scuff back to the road, and perch on some rocks next to the side heading back in our direction. Timon sticks his thumb out and looks towards the roundabout.

"We waited less than two minutes last time," giggles Naiad annoyingly. "I couldn't even -"

A car is already pulling up. Even though there are four spaces, we know immediately that we will be abandoned here with our walking carpet and our box of slowly heating beer and vodka. Timon winks like a gnome and gives a little shrug as he and Naiad jump in and speed off back to [location redacted].

I assume the position, whilst Mierda hides Grizzly behind a rock, before disappearing inside her phone.

We wait. A dozen or so cars pass, and I keep smiling and thumbing and smiling and sighing as they pass. It's hard not to hate the empty cars that roll by, hard not to calculate their carbon footprint bitterly and wonder at the selfishness of it all. Like squatting, hitch-hiking is a counter-intuitive process for most people, for whom convenience and entitlement go hand-in-glove. Sweat continues to slide down my spine. I keep checking the redness of my arms.

The first car pulls up, and I have that rush of relief and faith in humanity flush through me as I bound up to the window and break into my GCSE French – rusty from nearly two decades abandonment.

"Bonjour, m'sieur! Je voudrais allez [location redacted] – c'est deux kilometres a la droit. C'est possible?"

"Oui, bien sur!" says the young dark-haired gent manning the silver Citroen. He opens the door helpfully and I spin around to shout at Mierda and grab the box of warming beer. Grizzly

obediently staggers to her feet and heads towards the door, at which point I see the man's face fall.

"Tu avais un chien? Oh, je suis desolee -"

The door slams, the engines revs, the lift departs.

"Bollocks." I spit, regretting it immediately as my mouth is so dry. Inwardly, I curse Timon and Naiad's luck. "Your turn."

Mierda takes up the position, and I sit, hot and sulky, on a hot rock that grazes my arse.

I have barely begun complaining again when a second car pulls up – silver again, the wheel arches splattered with red sores of rust and the front crumpled and battered like a much-loved canteen. Inside, a huge sailor of a man sits hunched over the wheel, his face swollen with travel and excess and grey, smiling eyes peering out at us from bushy eyebrows like dancing caterpillars. Mierda whirls in a panic.

"George!"

"Just talk to him!"

Mierda has exactly two words of French, which she deploys immediately.

"Bonjour! Merci! Do you speak English?"

I am already behind with the box. *"Je voudrais allez [location redacted]."*

"Oui, bien sur, d'accord," he pops the doors.

"Avec le chien es possible?" I add. Grizzly looks up at him with her best hopeful smile, tongue hanging like a provocative piece of bacon from her maw.

"Mais oui!" rumbles the sailor, and delightedly we pile into the car, me in the front and the rest in the back.

The engine roars, and we are away.

The shibboleth of attempted French exchanged, the sailor introduces himself as Bastien, and switches to halting but comfortable English.

"You are staying at [location redacted]?"

"Yes, just for a day or two, we are passing through. We are

staying at Murat's place. The wood carver." Every time I say his name I can't help but mime the symbol for wood-carving, to my mind, a clenched fist held and tapped with an imaginary hammer. Murat's name again raises the dancing caterpillars up Bastien's face.

"Ah, *oui*. I live there as well."

"How-long-have-you-lived-there?"

"For five years now, but I am leaving. I want to go to a smaller place. I have a place the other side of Toulouse, with maybe five or ten people. Here, it is too many. There must be a hundred at times. There is too much story, too much -"

He shrugs, gesticulating with a pinched finger and thumb, winding upwards into the air like a conductor trying to time a tornado.

"*Je comprend*," I say, perhaps my favourite French expression these last weeks. "We lived in squats in London with 30 or 40 people and there is just too much story, too much drama."

"It is a shame. It is a good place here" – he says "ear" of course, being French, "but this is the life. Things must change."

"*C'est la vie*," I add, showing off just a little.

Within minutes, we have covered the four-kilometre odyssey we undertook in the mad-dog heat of the afternoon and swiftly turn off the main road, passing through the lane bordered with thick brambles hung with swollen sweet berries. My fingers are still stained purple from where we dallied earlier foraging for lunch. The temperature drops as we roll under the shade of tall trees, and suddenly the song of insects is all around us, the close rhythmic whisper of thousands of hidden creatures.

Bastien pulls into [location redacted], through the first gate of welded bicycles turned blood red with rust, like the capillaries of some bizarre organism preserved in formaldehyde and hung at the entrance. The second gate is an entire station wagon cut in half. We rumble past the reconstructed houses, the walls repaired with warped constructions of concrete and elaborate wooden panelling. We pass a JCB digger, painted green and half-swallowed by a spindly beech tree, a beer balanced on its trough; a turquoise green camper van, its roof bright with iron oxide, slumped in the grasses, a dog running after us barking in outrage as we pass; low cottages with terracotta tiled roofs, all manner of shapes and sizes of windows and frames cut into the side, no two uniform, all weird angles and twisted perspectives, creating the feeling that you are always slightly tripping when you look at it; in one yard a little mini boxcar in painted black with a flaming yellow hood; next to it, an abandoned car leans at a drunken angle on the slope, plastic tubing of green, brown, black, half-covering it like some futuristic fungal infection; everywhere bicycles stashed in bushes, cars half-hidden in the jungles, areas of plants and plastic-sheeted greenhouses hidden behind overgrown berry bushes and stands of sativa. Some cottages are hidden like guerrilla nests under a swathe of thick foliage, behind adorable gardens of marigolds and legumes. Others brazenly stand clear, painted with huge cartoonish murals of deviant mutants wearing boxing gloves. Everywhere there is something: old motorbikes and stacks of beer crates, bizarre metal sculptures and collapsing rooftops. There is a huge geodesic dome of white, and inside a cinema screen with leather sofas organised in expectant rows before it. One workshop's innards yawn open, and we can see worktables piled with intricately and gnomically sorted collections of trash, tools and litter, parts and scraps neatly ordered, everything filed with the dedication of the obsessive compulsive, the very walls inside painted with the inextricable madness of the organised hoarder.

We drive on, entering out into the field.

Here, the sun begins to drop, painting the circus parade of vehicles in lurid hues of orange and violet. There are trucks beyond number, organised into loose looping rows. Huge container trucks, Luton vans, camper vans, tractors, trailers, school buses, caravans, sharabangs, horse-drawn carts, mopeds, scooters. Every one of them is battered, or painted, or converted, or modified, or customised, hung with flags and stained with slogans, splattered with rust with home-made windows sliced into the flanks at different levels. Some are sunk into the ground, some propped up on bricks, some with lean-to shacks and raggle-taggle shelters built around them. Children run between them, and everywhere dogs peer curiously out from their various posts and territories, sniffing uncertainly as the car rolls by.

Bastien rolls us up to his huge container truck, easily ten-tonnes of domestic metal lying in the grass like a steel buffalo.

We shake hands and say merci, scampering away from Bastien with our supplies and heading back towards Murat's place, running the gauntlet of dogs that scurry out to greet us. Mierda keeps Grizzly on the leash, and each passing intruder I greet and keep at a distance with a stern but controlled "psssst", as if I am trying to get the attention of a drug dealer.

"This is the benefit of living in the mountains of India with packs of wild dogs," I brag. "Show no fear, Mierda, show no fear."

We meet Nookie by the compost toilets painted with radioactive signs, and she is chattering excitedly.

"I spent the whole day playing music with the kids," she gimbles. "There's a whole room full of pianos. Can you believe it? An entire room! The kids loved it, and Medusa loved it too."

Her one-year-old giant of a hound Medusa lopes along next to us, and leaps up when he sees me. I hold him on one arm and pretend to dance with him, a little interspecies waltz as we head back under the dusk.

We pass the *Metal Orgie* workshop – a hamlet of corrugated iron and twisted metal structures wrapped together in wood and paint, some freak hybrid construction with a huge railway bridge section arching over it.

"Where did they get a railway bridge from..?" wonders Mierda out-loud, but to no use. The treasures and wonders of [location redacted] have already overwhelmed us, and it now seems normal and natural that such a thing would appear here. At the top of *Metal Orgie,* a statue of a figure composed of bike wheels, chainsaws and a steering wheel peers inquisitively down at us, piloting his workshop to nowhere, a captain at the helm. We peer through the doors, and inside see the wooden skeletons of two old Roma caravans, naked and vulnerable, part way through refurbishment. Through the doors suddenly rumbles a rundown Jaguar car, no glass in the windows, a shirtless man with a mohawk and circle-glasses at the wheel, a map of the world tattooed into his arm. He waves cheerily at us as he passes in a cloud of dust and crackling stones. Nobody says "*Max Fou*" but we all think it.

We continue, reaching the field where the giant sienna horse grazes next to the little dwarf pony, fenced off seemingly by string. They gaze at us with solemn, hippoline knowledge and Nookie and Mierda pause a while to pet them and coo softly at their shaggy manes.

At the end of Terre Blanque, just before the woods begin, there is Murat's place.

Wierzbowski is shirtless, sweating in the garden, and waves to us as we arrive – a scarecrow of sinew topped with a tricolour dread hawk of fuchsia, scarlet and emerald, bundles of locks tied into horns of luminescent rope. The muscles of his compact frame move like rats in a bag as he ploughs through the wild garden fenced by overgrown lawnmowers and desiccated logs, stripping out unwanted plants by the root and gradually revealing the lattice of pumpkins, courgettes, tomatoes and ganja plants that are struggling their way through. A pile of discarded vegetation already lays by the path, ready for mulching. I inwardly wince as I see it, having worked for years on a philosophy of "do-nothing" gardening, whereby you never uproot a single plant, instead cutting it and laying it atop the soil to feed the others you wish to encourage. I say nothing, practising the ethos of non-intervention even here, knowing that it is never polite to intervene in someone else's garden.

Sweat runs down the sides of his face: a skull rictus of taut skin, rows of small tan teeth with gaps at the back, smiling as I hand him a gift of a bottle of vodka. He leads us back into Murat's shack, past the burnt-out rust corpse of an old van that lies half-swallowed by the bush, tall bamboo sprouts blossoming from its guts like some gigantic parasitic fungus that has consumed its host. A sign reading *"ZONE A RISQUE"* is propped above a limbless Greek statue sat in a wheelbarrow.

"Look at this man," he says, as we step between the bus and the shell of another van into the Crusoe shack Murat has thrown together from bamboo and random shanks of wood. He pulls a piece of camouflage netting off the bench, revealing a squat 18-inch cannon, the iron rusted to a blood red, the barrel pointed through the wall at the entrance.

He is chuckling with the fondness of mad friends. As well as the garden, whilst we have been away he has been tidying the shack, if such a thing is possible. The single room is open on one side, and filled with a mouldering mattress and futon around a low table. Shelves line two sides, with windows at the back almost blocked out by the bushes that press reassuringly against it. The shelves are filled with all manner of wood-carving chisels, stacks of chainsaws with rusted chains, rows of impeccably sorted spanners and wrenches of all sizes, incongruously clean and shiny amidst the dust and random assortments of lamps and wooden crates of spray cans, power cable extensions, broken amplifiers and bottles of anonymous liquids. One shelf is filled with pickled embryos, tiny closed-eyed kittens pressed into jars of brown formaldehyde, their little paws pressed yearningly against the glass, mouths aghast bearing teeth that will never grow. Another contains the coil of a thick black snake, forever frozen mid-strike, its venom fangs exposed for a kill that will never land. There are polished brass shell casings, one 18 inches long, gleaming in the setting sun next to a hand-held crossbow pinned to the wooden boards. Hung on one archway is the zombified remains of a steampunk cat, screaming at us with a World War Two medal covering one eye as a gothic metal eyepatch. Next to an angle grinder left on one bench is a box of bullets, some scattered haphazardly across the work surface. I pick one up and examine it.

"They are blanks," explains Wierzbowski, sitting taut and ready to pounce on the futon. He opens jars of pickled cucumbers and cracks a beer. Nookie is wheeling around confusedly, holding a bottle of vodka in doubt for a moment, before shoving it into the freezer compartment of the little fridge. Medusa bounces around dopily after her. "Ali! Ali!"

Wierzbowski shouts for the little puppy, Ali, who flops dutifully over to him.

At the same moment, I peer into another open box, and see the mummified corpse of a puppy not much younger than little Ali. It lies as if robbed from an Egyptian tomb, the eyes gone, but the skin of the face hard and preserved as old leather. The skin flakes like scales as it approaches the neck, becoming papery and delicate. One forearm only gleaming white bone, and the ribcage perfectly exposed like the ribs of a ship. It lies next to the bones of its tail, as if napping whilst awaiting its reattachment.

"Murat really is crazy, man," says Wierzbowski. "Even the kids were here earlier, telling me. They were saying to me ,'ah, so you are Murat's friend, ah? He good but he a little' -"

He waves his hand, spread fingers, next to his temple, eyes wide and smiling. "He tried to kill me once. But he tries to kill all the people he loves! He tried to steal my car one time, and I jumped through the front window with my legs sticking out in the air, and he just jumped on the accelerator. I had a single moment to decide, whether to hang on and probably die, or to let go there and then."

"What did you do?" asks Nookie, eating a pickle.

"*Korva!* I let go! I knew that he was not going to stop, so I had to let go! He came back later with the car and we laughed about it, but all his friends say it, that if he likes you he tries to kill you. He makes these knife handles like dragons, I never seen such detail in them, so much work man. Opinel knives. He buys them for nothing and then carves all the wood, sells them for like hundreds of Euros in the markets. Incredible stuff."

"How long has this place been going, do you know?"

"They been here about ten years. They have some sort of deal with the owner so they can stay. I was living at one old squat in [location redacted], but every weekend I used to come here for the parties. Amazing parties. Fakking amazing parties, man. I used to finish work on the Friday and drive straight up here. They used to drop me off Friday, pick up Saturday, then I'd be back Saturday night. Eventually they just dropped me Friday and I came back on the Sunday to go back to work Monday.

Wierzbowski scoops up the little goofy puppy and sits with it in his lap, idly rubbing its head as it tries to chew his fingers.

"But they all like that. It's too much, sometimes. The guys in [location redacted], this one old squat there, you walk in and there's this huge twin-barrelled machine gun sat pointing at the door. The one you can sit in, man. Take out fakking airplanes with it and it's sat right there, pointing at the door. They all fakking crazy anti-state anarchist mother fakkers. It was in Toulouse I skipped plastic explosives out of the bin. Fakking Semtex. I left it there, I didn't know what the fak to do with it."

As it gets darker, the mosquitos start to niggle and prance, so we fill up the steel drum with "Eat The Rich" cut into the side of it and set it alight. The lettering glows a satisfying insurgent orange and rebel red, the smoke choking off the worst of the mossies' attacks. We break out the vodka, by now super frosty from the fridge, and it starts to make steady circles around the group, each shot from the bottle matched with a sour crunch of gherkin.

"Polish-style."

"Ha. I know people that when they drink vodka, they just take the bread and rip it open and smell it."

Naiad and Timon join us, Mierda and Nookie not long after, looking refreshed from bathing in the burst waterpipe near the bridge in the forest.

"You guys, you all drink too much, it's too much sometimes, really," Nookie is saying, floating around drinking cider, harassing her clumsy giant puppy. "I still don't know what I'm going to do -"

"Fucking hell Nookie, just make a decision -" Naiad starts.

"But if I get in the van, I get in the van -"

It goes on like this, and other people, friends of Wierzbowski, arrive out of the dark and gather around the steel-can fire, moths drawn to the flame, warding off the darkness. I studiously and drunkenly scrape wood together, tinder dry from the relentless heat, and start a small fire in the clearing behind the shack. I load a grill on to it and diligently barbecue pumpkin, sausages, wrap potatoes in silver foil and shove them in the embers. By the time they are ready I will not be hungry any more. The vodka bottle circulates, and the night air fills with the mutant patois of Polish, French and English, rising up over the crackle of flames and the incessant buzzing insect chorus.

Later, we are out wandering amongst the vans, in a clearing amidst a dozen or so caravans, with smiling, clownish strangers laughing and rolling around us. One shirtless man has a fire staff, and is whirling it clumsily beneath the silver dollar moon. He drops it, flips it up with a foot, whirls once, drops it again. After the third or fourth time, I surge forward, collecting it in one hand and immediately beginning to spin it. My momentum is unsteady, wild, unfurling, and I dance beneath the moon. There is a shriek as I accidentally burn someone, but I do not stop. Someone emerges with a giant staff, three-flaming torches on each end, and they move as if an orchestra of flame, swirling glowing meteor slashes through the heat of the night.

Later still, we are cruising through the vans in an old car, driven by a stranger with a mohawk and circle-glasses, the engine purring and growling as he guns it through the near darkness. I have an impression we are driving to some guest quarters, hidden somewhere in the complex of buildings we explored earlier, but I never remember getting there, only waking up the next day in a tent next to Murat's shack, with Mierda sternly looking over me.

"You don't remember last night, do you?"

"Er."

"You burnt an old guy with the fire staff. He was obviously tripping his nuts off. He looked really upset, and suddenly said: 'I'm burnt. I have to go put something on it.' You were totally pissed. There was a girl doing a really good show behind you and you were ruining it."

"Ah well. It's important to get some practice. We're leaving today anyway."

"Before they kick us out."

"Why would they kick us out? We're adorable."

She laughs. "So you think."

"Someone has to."

6

Felicity J. Shit

Sometimes we have the absolute certainty there's something inside us that's so hideous and monstrous that if we ever search it out we won't be able to stand looking at it. But it's when we're willing to come face to face with that demon that we face the angel.
Hubert Selby, Jr.

The security guard returns day after day, banging on the door and moaning like a little bitch. After several mornings of this, I snap, and run down to the door to slam furiously against it:

"YOU FUCKING WANNA COME IN MATE? YOU WAMME TO OPEN THIS FUKKIN DOOR? I BEEN UP ALL NIGHT SMOKING CRACK! YOU WANNIN? I WILL GOUGE OUT YOUR EYES AND SKULL-FUCK YOU! IM FUKKIN READY TO ROCK! AM A FUKKIN VOODOO WILLY MAN!"

He did not continue to knock, but I heard muttering, backhanded comments as he retreated away down the street.

This is merely phase one of what I have since named: *The Crackhead Defence*. It is not a tactic to deploy lightly, and certainly not without commitment to the kind of gravel-voiced violent mania that needs to be conjured for authenticity.

Unless of course you really have been up all night smoking crack, in which case this demeanour should come naturally.

Phase two is to follow him out into the street, asking what he wants, can't he understand that people are living here now, inside this abandoned estate agent's awaiting demolition.

"It was my job to protect this building."

"Well it wasn't yours to protect. Times are hard all over. Do you think we want to live in an estate agents? Especially one that smells of ass and Gregg's the whole time? We got nothing against you, pal. We're desperate."

Phase 3, as it emerged, is to talk to the boss. His manager is a wizened slice of gristle with a shaved head and a dead-eye stare.

"Now get this," he growls. "I've got no interest in owning property or climbing above my class. I'm no bourgeois manager. I'm a worker and a striver and I'm going on holiday. When I get back in two weeks, expect the court papers. Until then, the place is yours."

I blink.

"Ok then."

Some days I would just sleep – trying to blend my consciousness with oblivion, with blissful escape from gutting despair like a cannon blast through the stomach, like a fish still breathing with its intestines half-out and pink and wriggling on the rocks, like a dog half-crushed by a lorry trying to scrape its way back to its master on the pavement. My huge, empty room, the dog shit arbitrarily scraped off the carpets and the smashed up cupboards dragged out and flung into the basement, is furnished with a single mattress, my ancient yet loyal blue backpack, and what most resembled a toast rack containing five books: *The Basketball Diaries, Requiem For A Dream, Blood's A Rover, The Malaya Trilogy* and *The Restaurant At The End Of The Universe.*

Not that I read. Each time I picked one of the books up, and could do little more than open it at random, read a sentence or two, then slam it shut with disgust. The days would tick by, and I would roll over and over in bed and pray for unconsciousness to sweep over me. Sometimes it came, at others, it left me to roll and think and sweat and stew in my rancid misery, fully aware of the futility of everything, fully lost in bleak, bleak nihilism. The universe cared not, the only things assured were death and suffering and disappointment, succulent turds of life to chow down upon, yes flecked with sweetcorn nuggets of joy but throughout you never really forget what you are tucking into.

We awake at 3am, Monday morning, the speed having run out from the day before, we had successfully fucked ourselves unconscious, but now inexplicably awake in the middle of the night at the dawn of a new week. We fire up the laptop, and whilst watching *The Wolf of Wall Street,* idly leaf through the collection of books, lapsing periodically into warm silent content as London slumbered outside, a rare calm descending upon us.

"I was having this fucked up dream that the Devil was trying to jerk me off. I managed to wake up before I came though."

"Ugh, people's dreams. Is there anything more nonsensical and subjective than someone telling you about their dreams? I mean, anytime anyone starts a sentence with 'I had a dream last night' you know you're in for a fucking boring few minutes."

"I thought the Devil image was quite nice."

"I bet you stole it. You never come up with anything original."

"I'm a non-fiction writer darlink, that's the point. As the man said, good artists borrow, great artists shoplift."

Mierda sighs.

"Ah, to sit in this awful mess and watch some shit on a dumb glass tube and feel fine about it. There's really nothing you have to do, ever. No cracking or scouting, wars and bullshit madness. Mastering the art of doing nothing."

"Which when you think about it, may be the hardest thing of all to do."

"I don't know how much time I've wasted on booze and fucking around. It drives me insane with anxiety sometimes."

"That's your conscience. Jim Carroll called it 'the dead speaking to us'."

"But don't you feel that? Don't you have that knowledge that yeah, one day we will be the dead. One day we will be the conscience speaking to others. And what will we be saying? Celebrating the narcissism and indulgence of pricks like these bankers? Slowly we rot." She puts on her guttural, grind core growl. "*Slowly we ro-o-o-ot.*"

"I'm trying to embrace it. Being an artist. Creating something that will stink up the joint still after I'm a smear on a worm's butthole. It doesn't take much."

"Just everything you got."

"But I never feel more alive than when I'm actually doing it. When I run off to the taxi rank to write, I feel free, but it's as if it's a dream. Like I'm wholly conscious and unconscious at the same time. Dead and alive, reading the words I'm writing back years in the future, talking about something years in the past, which actually may or may not have happened exactly how I describe it. I surrender. At least it's more than the meaningless gibberish we're normally subjected to. At least it has some basis in a reality, however relative that reality might be not."

"I feel the same when I paint. Not like all this advertising bullshit. Painting I feel like I'm hanging out with the gods."

"Who don't exist."

"But through doing that we get to create them. That's what all religion and art and 99 per cent of human culture is."

"Everyone loves a good story, and reality is frequently inaccurate."

"I'm aiming for scripture-pure veracity and scandal-rag content. It gives me some faith in the world."

"I like that about you, but you can't worry about the world. It's going to do us all in in the end."

"Nobody gets out alive. And the certainties are around that you'll probably regret a lot of it at the end, and you'll probably want a do-over. That's why Buddhism appeals to so many I think. Like you get more chances to fuck it up. I think that's another reason I write – you get to retrospectively relive moments from the past, and somehow, make more sense of them."

She pauses. "Do you want to come to my studio today?"

"OK."

So as 8am, Monday morning breaks over the grimy

multicoloured shambles of Shoreditch, we wake someone up and spill out of the house on our bikes, heading to the east, through Cable Street past the giant mural of the battle, past the studios looming on the junction, packed with illegal sublets, and turning on to the Commercial Road past the crumbling wreckage of the shopfronts of Slimehouse. We head further, through Canning Town's rambling warrens and the McDonald's with a row of police cars pulled up outside, queuing patiently for burgers. We head further, finally hitting the Barking Road, and turning off to Mierda's studio.

She opens the door for me into her world.

The floor is a riotous catastrophe of paints spilled and open containers, jade and ruby, firey reds and rotten purples, vermilion and aquamarine slices carving the floor between the debris of old brushes and spent cannisters. The walls are covered with grotesque pornographic alien vaginas, swollen naked obscenities and stylised pencil nudes. The far wall is dominated by a huge grotesquery bar scene, of drunken pirates and cackling whores and trans-gender third sexes with fake tits and tumescent crotch-bulges spilling drinks and snorting lines in some seedy pub. A martini glass slops on the floor, cigarettes slapped in groping men's faces, a debauched saturnalia in which all the characters look somewhat familiar. In the centre, I recognise Mierda, laying royal and queenly in a blue wig with smeared make-up, her legs boldly spread pointing her crotch at the viewer with bold defiance.

"Looks like our house."

Mierda smiles, giving away no secrets.

She set to work as I diligently pull up a space on the desk and DJ carefully selected songs one after the other whilst secretly mesmerised by watching her work. She seems part-dancer, part-painter, leaping and squatting to the music, balletic and raw, swinging between graceful strokes and intimate caresses on the canvas and savage attacks that splatter and drool sensuously over the layers of paint. After a while, I am inspired to share with her something.

"Do you want to hear a poem I wrote?"

She smiles. "Yes."

Twisted, blistered, hamfisted
Mutilated yet still cognitive
A sprawl of mutant indiscretions
Piled upon each other without end
Without sin, without realization
Every drug taken, every liberty taken
Abused, poisoned, misused, intoxicated
Needles out our eyeballs and between our toes
Stacks of fresh human meat
In the shopping centre rows

In the suddenly chilling darkness
I find myself surrounded by sweating, clammy flesh
Anonymous bodies, blank faces
Panting and spent
Drained of all emotion
All desire
All humanity
We look at each other and see
The mound of human debris we have become.
Empty vessels, bereft of God.
We dress, and shake hands. Awkward smiles.

After the orgy
After all those perceived moments of fleeting bliss
And ecstasy beyond comparison
Those strata of novae like super-pleasures
After every degradation possible
After we've done it all, seen it all, experienced it all

We walk out into the cold night street
We will find
That our world has become a wasteland
Our souls have become vacuums
And we are no more satiated
Than when we came in.

She works with steady rhythm and persistence, but before long I can no longer control my desire, and as soon as she is distracted I pull her towards me and kiss her deeply. I pull down her tights and she climbs on to me on the chair, and we desperately bounce and rock and gasp together for a fierce moment before she pulls off, my cum spraying against her thighs and my hand like oil paint against canvas as I collapse back on to the floor breathless and entranced.

"We should do this every day!" I gasp.

She smiles in agreement.

I wake up one morning in the corner of the downstairs room, alone again. The last thing I remember is trying to watch *Dark City*, coiled between Naiad and Mierda.

She is standing over me. Fury burns in her eyes.

"What the fuck is wrong with you?"

I blink at her, suddenly terrified of her boiling rage.

"What?"

"You don't remember last night?"

"What? No. What happened?"

"I'm trying to help you, and you are trying to get it on with my best friend."

"What? I don't remember that."

"You don't remember last night? I went and slept somewhere else as you tried to get it on with her."

"I don't remember. I don't remember anything."

She scowls, her gaze hitting me like napalm.

"Do you often get black-outs?"

"Yes. No. I don't remember. It's with speed and alcohol. My body keeps moving but my brain is completely absent. It's full on zombie style."

At the same moment, the doorbell goes and Mierda shoots me bullets of disgust with her eyes that poison my very blood. I turn, open the door. It is Naiad.

I spit it out with the shock of the recently wounded.

"Hey. Did anything happen between us last night?"

"Definitely not."

I am incensed with confusion and rage, and storm out the door for Naiad to lock it.

I storm through the streets, heading south towards the river, passing the huge Topps Tiles where I once spent the night taking MXC with Spike and hallucinating about naked Harlequin-women with triple-breasts and man-trap vaginas, before turning and heading east down the highway, past the Old Rose pub where I first saw Drowning Dog and Malatesta play with Bristol anarcho-hip-hop duo QELD. Around halfway down the road, I realise I am dressed in a leopard print woolly jacket, shirtless underneath, wearing an over-sized pair of aviator sunglasses and looking like the scum of Shoreditch reborn. I don't care.

I take my rage and confusion down to the park where me and Lice lay in each other's arms in the sun in the weeks before she left for France, never to return. She was out there now, living on top of a hill, tending a garden, like I used to with Ari, only a few short months before. I wondered what I was doing with all these frenzied chaos punks with their heartless casual sex and ill-defined relationships. In the pocket of the jacket, I find a scrap of paper with a fragment of Jim Carroll scrawled on it:

Little kids shoot marbles
where the branches break the sun

into graceful shafts of light…
I just want to be pure.

I cry, and then wrap myself in my leopard print jacket and pass out in the sun for a few hours sweet release, numbed to sleep by the steady drone of traffic on the highway.

There are 12 of us crammed into her tiny room in Dock Street, the dog under the massage table, the rats in the cage, the noise and chatter deafening. Awi is flailing around, bouncing into the table, beers slopping across the ash-stained carpet, the high-pitch mosquito whine blazing as Mierda commences carving the body of a triple-breasted naked woman with snakes for hair into my arm. The remains of the pen drawing are etched in triple colours of red, black and green, tentacles and the swollen knobbly testicle of the octopus' body covering the elbow. Fyodor and Ona and the others are gabbling, shouting, laughing and cackling, the noise deafening.

"What's the tattoo about?" Awi asks.

"It's about desirous attachment: the triple-breasted women are the embodiment of the impossibility of satisfaction with sexual desire – there are no perfect females to make everything ok. The octopus is the tendrils of desire itself – sticky, chameleonic, slippery, sneaky. They are masters of camouflage, of transformation, using ink and changing colour to hunt and survive. But they also regenerate – they heal, they regrow severed limbs. Is that line for me?"

We snort and the tattoo grows organically across my shoulder, finally extending a body to the disembodied Medusa-head begun years before in Malaysia – a stick-and-poke pinned over 24 hours by an interminably slow junkie who'd trained with all the time in the world, in prison.

It becomes too chaotic. Mierda wipes it off, and wraps it in clingfilm. We bump fists, and eat a wrap of MDMA we had saved, before heading off out to the party.

We jump buses with flashcards, sucking stolen bottles of port, snatching from shops on the way down to the Walworth Road, where Ona the Feral's house are celebrating their imminent eviction with a house party in an empty Chinese takeaway. Everything becomes patchy, incoherent. The rooms are filled with bodies slumped against one another, grinning and rolling with that inane Shulgin smile of false emotion.

I lose Naiad and Mierda somewhere in the throng, and before I know what is happening, I lose consciousness and reawake in the morning sun, unsure of what day it is. I stagger through the laughing folds of flesh and limbs, and somehow Ari is there, beaming and blue-eyed and beautiful as when I first met her, and we are holding hands in the sunshine and then we are kissing in the street, laughing into each other's faces, twirling and yearning and I am trying to pull her into the bushes, into the park, into secrecy, to get her to leave with me, and she is laughing and saying no, we're both on drugs. We want it to be real but we are both on drugs.

We have to stop. But we will meet. I ask her to come home with me. I am confused yet hopeful and thinking once again that maybe this is the person I'm meant to be with, maybe we can give it another chance, maybe all my decisions were wrong and it has been long enough. The garden is calling to me, the past is calling.

I promise to leave, and in a confused state wander the house somehow looking for Mierda and Naiad, but they are nowhere to be seen now. I find Ari again, and ask her to come home with me, not wanting to be alone. But suddenly they have to leave, someone has thrown a brick through the window of their squat, and they have to rally in defence.

I take the bus home alone, eyes rolling and mind fucked and feeling suddenly desperately alone, savagely horny, the ecstasy driving me into a frenzy. I get home, smash the door until Raitus opens it, dressed in lycra with his radio, ready to work. I stagger upstairs to claw at Mierda's door. It is locked.

I return to my lonely, empty room, sending her a text:

RU AWAKE?

As I wait for her to respond, I masturbate like a caged chimpanzee in a drugged rage at a vivisection lab. As I cum all over my wrist, my phone beeps.

WHAT?

I flick the spunk into an old sock, all my motivation drained out with orgasm.

JUST CHECKING YOU WERE HERE.

I pass out in confused misery. I cannot continue like this.

The day after the Anarchist Bookfair. I walk home, alone, savagely hungover, through the suddenly Sunday morning streets, after waking up alone on a crumbling sofa in the basement of Haggerston baths, abandoned again after another night of disastrous bouncing between incoherence and lust, screaming arguments in the bowels of the swimming pool with Ari, dribbling gibberish at Mierda, accidently kissing Naiad. Chaos. I must have been too drunk to be woken up, so they left me there.

At least I was NFA'd at Bethnal Green Police Station for greasing up that security guard on Jubilee Street. At least I got to see Peter Gelderloos talk about *The Failure of Nonviolence* yesterday. At least I still had my phone and wallet and a house to walk back to.

Least. Least. Least.

As I pass a church on Dalston Lane, the sound of an old timey organ building slow transcendent chords begins to build. I hear cheering and clapping echoing through the inviting door, and decide, fuck it.

Inside, in the cool arches of the high timber-frame church, the sunshine pours through a stain-glass window of a man with a halo crown atop a white horse spearing a twisted serpent beneath its hoofs. A tall black man with thick-rimmed glasses and a pompadour is standing in the pulpit ahead of a mass of people in their Sunday best, a pool of floral prints and clean-cut pastels, the air shimmering with hand fans. I slip into an empty pew to rest a little while and gather my thoughts. I hold the metal cogs tied to my denim jacket to stop them jangling. A few people look round at me and smile benevolently. I am the only white person in a crowd of around a hundred.

The man in the pulpit is testifying: "When I woke up this morning, I heard a disturbing sound. I heard the jingle-jangle of a thousand lost souls, seeking the divine light. But it's too late, too late, for them to seek what they might find. For the day of the lord cometh as a thief in the night."

The crowd is cheering, hallelujah and amen, brother. I hear the heartbeat bass and drum of funk rippling from the corner stage. The energy begins to build, people whooping and cheering and clapping, suddenly on their feet. One by one, chicken-stepping and punching the air as the tempo builds and the crowd raises their praises.

And in that moment, the sun blasts through a clear beam of light that pierces through the fog of my confusion, and I realise, lo, here I could find salvation and meaning with the happy-clappers and the God-botherers and the Jesus freaks, I could assign all my reason and confusion over to a book written by patriarchs and landlords hundreds of years ago, and now capitalised on by the cunning to fleece the weak sheeple and feed them false hope of a better life on Sugar Candy Mountain.

And I am up, and dancing and tapping my booted feet as the salvation surges around us, waving my hands in the air and whooping "hallejuah, brothers and sisters!", spinning in the aisle, for a moment leaping up on to the pew and considering throwing myself into the mass to crowd-surf towards the giant golden Jesus smiling from his cross at the end of the hall.

And then I realise:

"Holy shit, I must still be high as fuck."

I jump down off the pew and leave immediately, walking all the way back to Dock Street thinking, yeah, this is how the fuckers get you when you're down.

7

Lucifer's Invincible Summer

In the depth of winter, I finally learned that within me there lay an invincible summer...The only way to deal with an unfree world is to become so absolutely free that your very existence is an act of rebellion.

Albert Camus

Snowflake – of course Naiad called the van fucking Snowflake – Snowflake now glides through the Pyrenees – a moult of white sliding through the grey mountains, Naiad at the wheel humming Phat Bollard songs asking when are we gonna stand up and tell the government to fuck off. The road winds leisurely, and in the back a wave of seasickness settles over me, as if I am crossing some great, hot ocean. Through the windows, I glimpse the last villages of France as the rolling fields of Toulouse give way to severe sided monoliths of rock jutting arrogantly into the sky.

"They say when you cross the Pyrenees, you are entering into Africa. My home country," laughs Timon, shouting over the wind and the banging techno beats chuntering in the front.

"Well, we haven't crossed it yet."

I half slump, half hold myself against the rolling g-forces at the back, both holding on and letting go. We left Wierzbowski and Nookie in some suburb car park of Toulouse for them to make their way to his old squat with the little puppy, Ali. Nookie didn't seem sure what she was going to do up until the last minute; Wierzbowski already seemed at his wits end with her.

"She's fucking annoying me already man," he had muttered.

"Yeah, she struggles with decisions."

"Yeah, but that's not my fucking problem is it?"

Still, he had been too good hearted and too stoic to say anything to her, and had dutifully taken her off to be housed somewhere. I wondered where next she might turn up with her big lolloping dog. I hoped she'd be ok.

The air cools as we climb, and I peer out the side window at scraps of blue sky, trapped by solemn gravestones of mountain. I'd had doubts whether Snowflake would be able to make the climb over, but with Timon at the wheel, everything seemed relaxed and easy, and we cruised steadily higher into the sky and our next country of the trip.

"What the fuck is Andorra anyway?"

"It's a principality, like Monaco."

"Is it in the EU?"

"I guess."

"And who lives there? The Andorra-ites?"

"Andorrables."

"Andorristas."

"Andorra-explorers."

"Andorrans, you clowns."

We are heading there as it exists as a free town – tax-free petrol, booze and cigarettes – too good an opportunity to miss on our sprint over the mountains to Barcelona.

"Is that it? It's tiny?"

Andorra looks like an overgrown ski-resort, a ragged collection of commerce and car parks caught snug as a tick in the folds of the Pyrenees.

We miss the turn-off and roll around a giant roundabout three-four times before spotting the huge petrol symbol on a building carved into the mountain above us. Cruising up, we collect all the money we can to fill up Snowflake and the giant plastic barrel we have brought with us. The attendants are helpful and polite, rushing through a steady flow of cars from France, Spain, Italy and beyond that are queuing to take advantage of the tax haven.

The van pulls in, and we leap out into the car park carved into a precipice overlooking a quaint stream that runs through the jagged barren vectors of the mountains.

At the apex of a narrow valley, some callous architect has slung a bunch of cast-off shopping malls, car parks and budget hotels with grimy neon signs. On the hill, a vast lego-brick construction of cyan and budgerigar yellow is festooned by frozen cranes, parked next to what seems to be the Biggest McDonald's in Europe, five floors of Big Macs and heart disease. The outpost is deceptively small and compact, a blemish of consumerism in grey and tan dwarfed by the bleak barren greens of the moors around it. Off down the valley, the soaring lonely mountains huddle, slowly creaking in the heat.

"They're not big on trees here, are they?"

We stroll up the hill, into the outpost. People in shorts and sunglasses are wandering to and fro over the giant roundabout, carrying boxes filled with huge bottles of liquor and cartons of cigarettes.

I pause. One car, metallic sky blue, has had its back window smashed. It has Andorran plates. As I look closer, I see in the front windshield a constellation of small, perfect holes. The front passenger's headrest is smashed to pieces, just two bars of shiny steel poking up from the seat. In the boot, I see another collection of finger-sized holes.

"Bullet holes." I point them out to the others. "Where the fuck are we?"

"I suppose people bring their cars here to dump them. Andorran police can't be all that much."

I stare for a while, imagining high-speed pursuit up the mountains, people driving hard and fast, escaping cops or robbers, on the run from some bank job or jewellery heist. Someone would be adrenaline-flushed having narrowly avoided getting their head blown off. I daren't look closer to see if there are blood-stains.

There are restaurants advertising extortionately priced food, jewellers and pharmacies and a pet shop and a lingerie store. We pass a hunting and weapons store selling mock-up guns, fishing gear, knives in all shapes and sizes, katana, nunchaku, throwing stars, hunting jackets and smoke bombs. Naiad runs in excitedly to buy pepper spray.

"What for?" asks Mierda.

"Perverts."

"Better watch out, Timon." We smile. We are delayed whilst Mierda is looking at leatherman tools for her tattoo gear, but she decides they are all cheap shit. Whilst we were distracted, we lose Timon and Naiad, but head to the superstore anyway.

When we emerge 20 minutes later, we are laden down with gigantic bottles of vodka, gin, pastis, absinthe, packets of tobacco, papers and filters, and we stagger down towards the van. Naiad rejoins us, carrying a box of beer, Timon with a carton of rum.

"The prices," she stammers. "The prices could drive you crazy. I stood in the aisle not knowing what to take."

"This rum," says Timon. "This is the special from my island. You cannot buy like this anymore. They stopped it. Made it less strong. Look at this box – so broken and old. This is a relic!"

We stagger down the hill, pausing at the Andorra sign to take a photo of us with our loot, feeling like freebooters pouring out into some musty pirate's den to spend our ill-gotten gains. We raise the bottles above our head in salute to Andorra, stickering up the sign with our various signs, before rolling back down past the shot-up car to the van.

"Funny thing about these isolated spots -"

"- tend to be difficult to get to."

We trek through the sandy pines lugging our five litres of water, our busted-up parasol, our bags of booze and potatoes, stumbling and chatting. El Culo skips ahead, lean and light-footed, Timon and Naiad behind us, me, Mierda and Grizzly spread in between, thorns scratching our bare-legs and feet skidding in the dust. The forest sings around us, a million cicadas thrumming orchestral polyrhythms together. For a while we are lost, but spot wandering bevies of tourists clad in summer get-up rangale-ing through the slim trunks that help us guide our course. Seagulls shriek unseen above, and after an hour, a sea-breeze of salt and spume begins to cool the sweltering closeness of the woods.

The pines break, and beyond, we see a twin layer of beryl and indigo above the tan rocks. As we reach the precipice, there is a sign that reads: Waikiki Beach. Platja Naturista. There are crude drawings of bikinis and speedos with red lines drawn through them. It is hung below a metal, official sign that informs us in no unclear terms that if we should fuck up here, we will not be rescued.

The beach is a tusk of ivory below, curved between the sheer drop of the rock and the wild tumult of cusping waves that ceaselessly beat against the shore. Bodies are strewn across the sands as if washed ashore, pink and brown and fleshy like mutineers collapsed in the surf. Couples promenade delightfully naked through the surf, and in the waters more figures gambol, shaved apes in sunglasses.

We scale down the rocks, into the mix, and find a spot between nude bodies. Tits and bits and cocks and no socks everywhere. A young couple like gazelles play beach tennis, swinging body parts through the breeze. We are greeted by curious bovine stares as people watch our arrival expectantly. Not wishing to disappoint, we strip and reveal to the beach what we be packing.

We set up the broken parasol as precariously as possible to heighten the excitement of possible impalement, laying the towels around it before taking turns to sit drinking on the beach, or plunge into the aggressive waters to frolic and feel each other up, disappearing around the rocks for secretive, furtive explorations and adventures.

Crabbling about in the bushes, Mierda finds a bomb. An actual bomb. It's pale cream like a bleached coconut, smooth and polished, the size of a honeydew melon, with a liquorice red fuse protruding from the top, sealed with wax. We debate whether and when to set it off, but as we drink more, the thought of blowing holes in the sand and blasting limbs off bodies deters us. We hide it in a bush again, for some lucky children to find, or some local guerrillas to seek out.

In the distance, gigantic chimeric tankers hover like distant islands, half-hidden in the haze, ghostlike reminders of the industrial nightmare just over the horizon. Grotesquely huge metal behemoths, they lurk, ever present, whilst the colony of nudists lounges and lazes in the torrid Mediterranean sauna.

We get lost in the woods for some time, missing the turn-off and wandering through the sweltering pines, deafened by the constant roar of cicadas in the brush.

"They throw their voices you know," I am saying, half-delirious. "You can never find them. In India, where I lived, the forests were like this. One summer they all hatched, or shed their skin, and the forest was full of millions, literally millions, of little carapaces. Little skins, perfectly preserved, that they'd popped out of and abandoned. Everywhere. Every inch of the floor crunching underfoot as you stepped. The dogs used to eat them."

We stagger on, every metre peppered with querulous snaps as we hit a fence marking the edge of a tourist concentration camp. Beyond the wire, little rows of hamlet huts house families preparing huge quantities of food, sandwiches, barbecues, all saggy bellies and wrinkled skin, doe-eyed children staring out at us as we stagger past like forest beggars.

The fence loops around, and we argue about which direction we came from.

"I don't remember going up a hill."

"You were drunk."

"True."

Finally, we pass the Espacio de Caca, the rich fumes of tourist-dung wafting on the stale breeze, and hit the roadway we were on the day before. Past the plundered blackberry bushes, under the railway tunnel and through the police line back to the searing griddle of the highway.

We dodge a few screaming cars and stagger back to the van. Naiad and Timon are already up, pottering about making coffee and chirruping at each other like merry sparrows.

"Did you clean Guadeloupe?" asks Mierda.

Naiad mutters something, eyes dodging away.

"It was horrible. I could barely stand it."

Mierda opens the cage. I sit in the heat, trying to breathe.

She returns in tears.

"She's burst, oh fuck, George what should I do? Should I have her put to sleep? It looks so bad. You have to help me decide."

Previously with all the rats, we had always decided to let them die of natural causes, not to foreshorten their lives and to keep them as alive and well as possible. The vets had explained to us that operating on them could kill them, that all rats get tumours, and that they have an inordinately high pain threshold, designed to prevent them from being picked off by predators when they look weak.

Fat Guadeloupe was only a year old, a birthday gift for Mierda, a dumbo pig with huge drooping ears and a round little face like a tiny white buddha with a tail. When she'd arrived she'd sat almost immobile in the top of the cage for four days. We were worried she was defective somehow. But eventually she'd started running around the barricades with the others, and become a firm favourite, with her own theme song and anime-like idiosyncrasies. A few months ago, she'd developed a tumour the size of a golf ball under one armpit almost overnight. We'd taken her to the vet, who'd said the usual, tested it for cancer. It was benign, but was only going to get bigger. Over the month, it had swollen exponentially, stretching the skin to bursting point, the fur parting and red sores blooming. We'd been cleaning it daily, and she had seemed happy enough.

"Let me have a look."

I climb up into the van, and unlock the cage. Guadeloupe is in the tiny toy fire station, and clambers out when I call her by name. Carefully, I reach inside and she climbs obediently into my hand. On first look, you wouldn't see anything wrong.

Then the smell hits me.

Rancid meat sweating in a bin in a back alley of Barcelona; rancour and corruption. Flies are strumming the air, seeking out the rot. She wiggles a little as I turn her over.

The tumour has burst, as if an explosion has torn half of her flank open, exposing vivid coils and craters of broken flesh, visceral rouges and purples, rimmed with creamy pus. I can look for no more than a second before I have to put her back in, disgusted and ashamed at my reaction.

I leave the van.

"It's time for her. We have to put her to sleep. She's going to get maggots. Which would actually be good, as they'll eat the rotting flesh. But I don't want that to be my last memory of her. And she isn't going to get better. Maybe if we were at home. Maybe if we didn't have to live in the back of a van, travelling through a super-heatwave. But this is it."

Mierda looks at me, tears in her eyes. I swallow my emotion as best I can. I have just pronounced a death sentence.

The second we drive to is in some anonymous barrio of some anonymous Catalan town, and we are greeted by a pair of adorable female vets, one of whom speaks enough English to follow what we are saying.

Mierda is cradling Guadeloupe. The second time we took her out she hadn't wanted to leave the little toy fire station, and had stayed in, ignoring her name, eating her last meal of cheese, studiously nibbling each piece of cheese with her nimble hands. Eventually, once she was ready, she had emerged, and Mierda had wrapped her up in a piece of cloth and held her to her stomach as she carried her out down the Green Mile.

"She had a tumour. We are travelling. We need to put her to sleep."

The vets at first seem sceptical. "It does not work like that here. First we have to examine and determine."

We hand over Guadeloupe, and the dark-haired vet opens the cloth, and immediately they realise why we are so certain.

"It is a tumour. It has burst."

They know immediately that there is no surgery, no chance to operate, no chance to save. They move quickly, yet kindly, on to the subject of euthanasia with the tone and deliberation of undertakers discussing the details of the funeral. They explain how it will work as Mierda holds Guadeloupe and I stroke the tiny white head, marked with a single patch of brown between the winking pink eyes. I am thinking of when I went to collect her from the pet shop in Lewisham, carrying her home in a box like she was a Faberge egg, terrified of stumbling and dropping her. I'm thinking of her growing fat and ridiculous, affectionate and responsive, as we slept under barricades in Southwark awaiting the bailiffs.

"What's her name?"

"Guadeloupe."

The Catalan Catholic girls cannot help but smile.

We nod in acquiescence, numb, distant. I am wiping tears, turning away to read about dog nutrition, examine charts on cat obesity, peer intently at miniature plastic models of healthy teeth and fangs. Occasionally I will gasp and stutter a little, seeing Guadeloupe's inquisitive little face peeping out from between Mierda's comforting hands.

Mierda holds her in the box gently, and Guadeloupe emits a

brief shrill cry as the vet gives her the first shot, an anaesthetic, that will numb her.

The impact is immediate and shocking. Guadeloupe all but disappears, becoming a zombie, mute, unresponsive, eyes open and staring, but now numb. It is like she is already dead, but still here, trapped in purgatory. Mierda signs the euthanasia papers, and I am relieved it is not my signature going on there to condemn our little friend. I remember the burst innards, I think about maggots wriggling in there, I think about doom and suffering, wiping guilty tears from my oily face.

After a few whispered goodbyes to what now feels like nothing more than a stuffed toy with a heartbeat they take Guadeloupe into a surgery room that is all white and hospital blue, tubes and mysterious machinery, overhead lights and sterility. We have to wait outside. We watch from the doorway as they lay her down on a clinical white table and place her head and nose into a plastic tube. They are giving her more anaesthetic, gassing her to completely knock her out. From this angle, you cannot see the ruin of her flank, and she looks as if she is undergoing some strange abduction by curious aliens in scrubs.

I do not watch as they administer the final shot, instead suddenly finding myself fascinated by charts measuring the correct weight of dogs. I wonder about Grizzly's weight. Perhaps we should feed her more.

We wait next to the desk in reception, and they bring out a large cardboard box, sealed with tape, and the vet places it down, and taps it two times reassuringly, as if carefully checking she was actually dead in there.

"This is always the hardest part of our job," says the vet, in a purring Catalan accent. "That will be 33 Euros."

Iberia is burning. As we drive through scorched earth carved with geometric lines of tortured olive trees, twisting from the cracked substrata like phalanx of calcified Methuselahs marching towards the naked mountain rock, plumes of smoke rise from the hillsides. Everything is burnt ochre, tawny with dust and ash, sun veiled sepia in a sky like a palette of opal and shit.

The van rolls on endlessly, a meagre breeze flapping the leopard print curtains of the back windows as we bounce and swing, bounce and swing, nauseous and breathless in the back. This fucking van, this fucking road, now approaching 7000 kilometres across Europe.

"Heatwave Lucifer, they're calling it," I talk, to distract myself from the sweat. "Heatwave fucking Lucifer. Like, hell on Earth, right? I mean, that's the implication. I read that in Iraq birds are dropping out of the fucking sky. Blomp. There's an eagle. Blomp. There's the vulture that was going to eat it, but oh, it's cooked in the fucking sky.

"Like, how long till the oceans boil up all the rest of the fish? You ever see a lake go rotten? Thousands of fish popping up to the top, goggle-eyed and gasping, washing up one after the other on the shore and everyone just sat there, staring at them, going 'oh fucking dear'."

We are rolling through a small town, lurching sickeningly sideways in the back as we hit the sharp curves. Old folks are wandering seemingly aimlessly through the streets between their low tan casas with the red-tiled roofs and charming shutters on the window. There are bunting and streamers hung drop dead still in the no-breeze, as if frozen, gay colours of some fiesta. Behind the houses, on a scrap of forest bleached to olive grey by the heat, the lick of flames beneath the boughs is visible, and columns of smoke coil upwards into the sky.

"You know what? All of this used to be forest. All of it. Like forest like we saw in Bialowiesca, like you have in Lithuania. Pines and oaks and beech and elm and yew and ash and all those. Diverse as fuck. You remember the soil I was pointing out in Hambach? Where we had the shitty picnic? Well, this whole area probably had as good if not better as that. Rich and fertile and healthy, five metres thick or more I bet. Wolves and deer and beaver and possum and squirrel. Then you know what happened?"

Helicopters are swinging through the clouds over the glow of the flames, spurting out a brief, spasmodic ejaculate of white into the boiling clouds with an audible whoosh. Up the hill, between the casas and the groves, we can see shapes in copper hats and umber jackets moving amidst the torched bracken and ash.

"The Spanish Armada. In the 1500s, they chopped down everything. Razed it. Built the biggest mightiest fleet of galleons and caravels and sloops and whatever the world had ever seen. Massive, hundreds of warships, thousands and thousands of trees. Everything. Slice-slice. Chop-chop. To the ground. They set off to invade merry old England, a war of succession, the big nobs off to war. Decades of preparation, the beginning of a boss power move to end all the imperial bickering and shut down upstart Albion for good."

Mierda is half-listening. I am half-listening to myself. The road rolls, a gunmetal snake coiling through the bronze wasteland.

"So off they pop, sailing off up the Bay of Biscay, ready to stomp, smash, kill, crush, destroy. And what should happen?"

I jam the window open full-blast to emphasise. We are moving at pace, and the wind whistles through, flapping the curtain violently in our faces.

"GEORGE!"

"They were chased by little English ships, speed over size, until they had gone almost right around England, up to Scotland, where they fucked up the navigation, and smashed most of their ships into the damn rocks. Nature smashed them up. Storms and heavy weather and the big wooden boats blasted on to the rocks by the North Sea. More people died from weather than from combat.

"Philip of Spain wept when his armada went down, was he

the only one to weep?

"Meanwhile, despite thousands of drowned soldiers, the Spanish had managed to turn their country into a desert. They'd be dependent on their colonies for years afterwards. Plundered silver and brazilwood, the riches of the New World, because they'd pillaged the old."

To our right, a great gathering of people in bright colours are dancing together beneath the bunting, and in a flash we glimpse a great coherent pattern of movement, of smiling faces and laughter, of clean pastel dresses and hands raised in union, of men with short neat haircuts and the rumble of a great ragged cheer of many voices raised in celebration.

Then it is gone, and after a few more houses, we depart the town and roll back into the wasteland.

"It's absurd. It's all so fucking absurd."

"Camus had something to say on that. He set absurdity between two other philosophies. Satre's existentialism: the creation of our own meaning in life, humanity's innate ability if not responsibility to auto create meaning. Nietzche's nihilism: that there is absolutely no meaning to anything in the universe, and indeed, all efforts to create one are futile. He fitted absurdity right in between. That we must create meaning, even in a meaningless universe, and the greatest quality we can attain in that pursuit is that of defiance. To defiantly create meaning in a world where there absolutely is not any."

"He was a goalkeeper for Algeria, you know."

"And David Icke for England, so there's absurdity for you."

"You heard this? Petrol truck exploded in Pakistan. Turned over in the road, petrol pouring out the side. People go nuts. The local villagers all running over, riding over on mopeds, scooters, bicycles, everything. Hundreds of people, bringing their grandparents, grandma, kids, all carrying plastic bottles, jerry cans. Police rock up try to keep them out, barriers up, but it's useless, they're unstoppable. A real party. I guess free petrol is a lot for people like this. And then -"

"Don't tell me."

"Nothing ever burns down by itself -"

"- every fire needs a little bit of help..."

"And then, someone lights a cigarette."

"Oh no."

"Poof. 212 dead. 212 dead, fuck knows how many injured. Fireball. Incinerated mopeds, cars, people, cops -"

"Not all bad then."

We start singing: "Give the anarchist a cigarette. The times are changing but he just forgets -"

"Nothing ever burns down by itself -"

"- every fire needs a little bit of help..."

"Fucking hell. Fucking people. Fucking world. Why do I get the awful feeling that this won't be the last petrol riot massacre we hear about?"

"Or food, or water..."

"At least that's not so explosive."

"Nothing ever burns down by itself -"

"- every fire needs a little bit of help..."

We lurch around another sharp bend, books fly from the shelves and we scream and swear as we are thrown into the spice rack, as Grizzly slides from the bed, as we stagger on to the floor.

"Fucking hell Naiad!"

"Hey!"

"Sorry!"

8

Shit 101

> *The outlaw anarchists shot at the police and blew out their own brains. Others, overpowered before they could fire the last bullet into their own heads, went off sneering to the guillotine...It was like a collective suicide.*
>
> Victor Serge

Giles arrives in his overcoat with his shirt casually open at the collar. Me, Awi and Fyodor are there to greet him. We have been busy all morning unhooking the custom-made circuit board and fuse box from the basement, clearing up the bits and pieces perpetually strewn across the floorboards, lumping bags of trash out the door on to Borough High Street, the intention is to make a good impression.

"Ya. So we have had squatters in this building five times. Each time in between stages of the refurbishment. It used to be an English school. Building belonged to my father. Last time we cleared it out to remove all the asbestos. Put an alarm system in. Squatters came round, removed the alarm system out the window to the security, and then obviously decided they didn't like the look of it, so left. Never bothered with the security after that."

I pull a face at Awi over Giles's shoulder as he slowly sojourns through his building.

"Well, we are very keen to work with owners to get a secure place to stay, especially as winter is coming."

"Ya." Giles's shoes are very shiny, and seemingly repel the dust that swirls up from the yawning gap-toothed floorboards with the ease of privilege repelling difficulty. "So every time I made a deal with the occupiers: no candles, it's too dangerous with all the wood here, and don't use the electricity, it's all stripped out. A neighbour called and said they saw lights in the windows. So no more candles."

"We use leisure batteries, we charge them at a friend's place and bring them back here, look." Awi has even rigged up one of the little portable batteries to a multi-socket, and as he plugs it in, an incongruous banker's lamp pings on, illuminating a dusty floorboard. Giles stares at it, like the butler just showed him some common rural magic trick.

"Ya. OK. Also, this wood panelling. It's vintage, antique, very expensive, and it cannot, absolutely cannot be damaged. It was all covered up before."

The huge wooden panels line the stairwell that coils up through the centre of the five-story building.

"We will take good care of them," says Fyodor. "We have no interest in damaging them."

"Another thing, someone said that they heard drumming in here?"

Me and Awi shoot eyes at Fyodor. He and Sasha had already set up all the music equipment in the basement downstairs. He smiles. He is missing his front tooth. It has a charming effect.

"Er, yeah, some of us are musicians," he beams.

"But we are happy to keep the noise down," jumps in Awi. "We don't want to upset any neighbours."

"Well, actually," says Giles. "If you want to play, then play at night-time, after office hours. It's all offices on either side, so if you keep it to night-time, nobody will ever hear you."

"Bonus," I say.

"We can definitely do that," says Fyodor.

"Ya, OK. Well, here's the deal. You do these things, let me check from time to time, and allow access, and I will give you as much notice as I can to leave. It'll probably be around Christmas, possibly the new year, but no later than that I imagine. I'll be able to give you around a couple of weeks' notice, but not much more than that."

"Two weeks sounds great. Christmas sounds great," says Awi. "We just ask that if you want to come around you give us 24 hours' notice so we can tidy up the place and have it nice for you."

"Ya, ya. That's all fine. I can take your numbers. So look, we can do all these things. But also, I can get heavy. Now I don't want to get heavy, but you know..."

Giles trails off, shooting us with his eyes like grouse from the skies over his family seat.

Awi has never looked more innocent.

"We have no interest in it getting heavy. We really appreciate you making an agreement like this. It makes a huge difference to us."

Giles eyeballs us, closing in on the art of the deal.

"Very well then. We have an agreement."

He puts out a manicured hand, and we have a home for the next three months.

Mierda, our guide and fearless leader, Daigas and Ona the Feral, Sasha and Naiad push seamlessly through the barriers at Waterloo to catch the last train heading west. To celebrate, we have decided to go to Thorpe Park for Halloween.

"I went there two years ago," Mierda pronounces it, adorably, "Thrope Park". "But I had taken *way* too much speed and the security caught us. I ended up biting one of them in the arm. They had like the perfect imprint of a bite-mark there. In the morning, they had my real name and everything, so there must be biometric information recorded somewhere as I've only ever given that stuff for my passport and ID. I was never arrested before."

"OK," I say. "So we try to take a little bit less speed, but enough to get in."

"Right."

"OK. Who's up for an adventure?"

We pass the vodka back and forth, a crew with a mission for the night.

We ride the nearly empty train, ever cautious for inspectors, passing the bottle back and forth and grinning and giggling together. London drops away, the noise and the tumult, the high-rises and the rows of suburban houses giving way to increasing stands of trees and spacious fields. At the stop, we jump out, we have made the first stage.

In the eerie calm of outer London, the moon burns hot in a hollow sky, casting glum pale shadows over the boughs of tall trees. The car park is desolate and empty, an expanse of glacial tarmac between us and the distant signs above the ticket gates that read THORPE PARK. Behind them, the shadowy skeletal bones of amusement dinosaurs soar and fall. We hear the distant clatter bang and laughter of the VIP crowds that have paid the extra to remain there for late night Halloween adventures.

We turn sharply to the right, and head off down a road into increasingly thick and dark forest. I am already drunk, wearing a Lucha Libre mask inherited from Osmond, and on the slip road as we head in, I decide now is the perfect time to take that last tab of acid I have been carrying the whole summer.

In the meagre light of the moon, I unwrap it carefully from the foil. It must be less than a quarter.

Whoosh.

A sudden breeze whisks it away. In moments like this, there is always the terror of forgetting you have taken acid, or, that you have not taken acid, but think that you have as reality starts to really fuck with you. Later I am to be extremely glad of this, and in my drunken state I simply curse, look briefly and in futility on the ground for it, before hurrying on to catch the others.

"So the park is on some weird like island thing, but it's connected to the land by a small part," says Mierda.

"A peninsular," I offer.

"Yeah, whatever, so we have to go around and sneak in through the back. Ready?"

We all nod, and head off, finding the service entrance road that curls around the side into deeper and deeper forests. The trees loom higher and more mysterious overhead, the bush growing ever deeper.

"I think it's here."

We plunge into the undergrowth, picking our way between thorn bushes and dense copses, Mierda following some almost unseen path. We reach a wooden fence, and find a gap that has been torn open in the side by previous adventurers. One by one we squeeze between broken, mouldering boards, avoiding the hang-nails, sweeping the leaves from our faces. On the far side, the grasses grow up to our waists and the branches snag at our clothes as we push deeper and further. Boots sink into thick humus and drag through snarling ferns. We stumble and laugh and occasionally stop to pass wine bottles around before pressing onwards. The forest clears a little as the slopes rise upwards and roll down, and seemingly we are lost for moments in some vast jungle, heading further from civilisation and the beaten trail, deeper into the unknown behind Mierda.

After nearly an hour, we stumble suddenly back on to a road, and see the lights in the distance of the theme park's security gates. Here, we slip silently across the road to a chain link fence. Eagerly I attempt to climb it, coiling fingers through the mesh and hurling myself heroically upwards. As I do, the mesh immediately collapses, unlinking from the flimsy posts and I collapse face first into the thick summer grass beyond.

"Go! Go! Go!" whispers Mierda hoarsely, and I scramble to my feet to chase after the others as we flee the lights splashing on to the road and into the meadows beyond, keeping to the shadows of the sparse brush and trees beyond.

"Are there cows here?" asks Daigas, looking a little concerned.

We are now less than 50 metres from the security post with

its floodlights and the towers of the park beyond. Mierda and Naiad are in the lead, and nonchalantly they stroll past the single wooden barrier, and into the park beyond.

Daigas and Ona the Feral follow, with me and Sasha the next pair, walking coolly but firmly past the empty booth, and into the park beyond.

At night, the dead theme park seems strangely similar to the forest. We walk the pedestrian ways, but then spot a miniature knock-up of an old school bus and some other vehicles, which we climb noiselessly inside to sit and drink wine.

We are all grinning at each other. "We're in."

We decide to try and head a little deeper in, and crawl out of our hiding space, heading further into the park. Overhead, metal creepers whirl and wait expectantly for the life that morning will bring, the steel bones of megafauna amusements. I am star-struck, ambling towards the rear, and suddenly need a piss.

I turn, and scuttle under a metal brace to relieve myself. This is great.

When I turn back around, everyone is gone.

Initially, I was not so concerned, and continued to amble around checking out this and that.

But suddenly I am confronted by security, two guys in hi-viz, strolling nonchalantly through the park, the fierce orange coats warning me like the stripes of a luminescent tiger.

I turn and run.

Running, running, running through an almost deserted theme park, I feel like some startled deer fleeing a lion in the forest, and for exhilarating minutes I feel my legs pounding and no sounds of pursuit behind me. I slow, taking a moment to look around.

Beside me is the derelict mock-up of a school bus again. Ahead, the little security station. There are now two security people there as well.

One of them smiles at me. I smile back.

"Hello there!"

"Hello. I'm a little lost. Where's the hotel?"

"Back there mate. You ok?"

"Sure I'm just looking for my friends, other way you say -"

"Yeah that's right. Can we just have a little look at your ticket -"

And I'm off, the deer is flying, I leap the barrier heading now back out of the park, now they are in hot pursuit, but I am relentlessly pounding my way down the road to freedom, driven only by the necessity to get the fuck away from people in hi-viz, the fuck away from authority. I glance around, they are heading back, fleeing away from me and back into the park. I realise what for.

I fling myself into the bushes, lying prostrate and prone under the brush by the road, breathing heavily. My phone buzzes.

MIERDA:

WHERE DA FOK RU

ME:

Security found me. I hiding in bushes.

A moment.

MIERDA:

DELETE ALL MSGS

ME:

OK.

I trawl through my phone, furiously deleting, until it's clear.

As I delete the last one, I hear the sound of a car crawling down towards me, the sound of rubber crushing gravel, the purr of a motor. I am being hunted.

First the headlights flood the bushes and I freeze like a startled rabbit, letting the light wash over me. Moments later, the roving beam of a torchlight joins, sweeping across.

Then it passes, switching to the calming red wash of the tail-lights.

I've done it. I've dodged the bastards.

But now what.

I lie there for some moments, feeling my heart pounding in my chest and my breathing gradually subsiding. I reach for my phone, about to text Mierda, when I hear them coming back.

The same wash of headlights, the same roving spotlight, but this time, it stops right on me.

"You alright there mate?"

Bugger.

I leap to my feet, brushing myself off.

"Hello there. I'm just looking for a place to sleep. I got a bit lost."

"This is private property. You can't sleep here."

"Oh. I see."

"Do you want to come with us?"

Not really. "OK."

Two hours later, they walk me out of the front doors of Thorpe Park and point out the bus stop where I am to spend the night waiting for the first bus back to London. The security guards were gentle enough, if a little incredulous as to the story I'd woven.

"I'm just up from London, looking for a place to stay. It's too violent in the city."

"Can't you stay in a hostel?"

"Too much drugs and violence. Even sleeping on the street is too risky. I prefer it out here. But I think I got lost somehow and ended up on your road there."

"Right. Well the police are on their way."

"Fair enough. I think I haven't really done anything wrong. Trespass maybe. A civil offence, not criminal."

"Well we'll see when they get here."

They offer me some jammy dodgers and a cup of tea whilst I wait.

The police arrive. Out of London cops always seem that little more ovine than bovine, and that's fine.

They looked through my phone, checking the messages.

"So we're going to search you, do you have anything on you that you shouldn't have."

"Nope, it's all fine."

"You were seen on CCTV with several other people in the park. Where are they?"

"I'm here all alone, officer. Just another wandering hobo type looking for a safe place to crash. I don't know anything about any other people."

They search me. The familiar pockets turn out and rifling through the bag. They are curious about a set of keys.

"It's for a little house I used to live in. Not anymore."

The police search me, and eventually shrugged and the security guards shrugged and I shrugged and there was nothing that anybody could do, so they led me outside and across the car park, gave me back my keys and my bottle of red wine and left me at the bus stop – the last bastion of shelter for the homeless. Of course, it began to rain, and Mierda rang.

"So what are you doing? Come back inside."

"No. No, it's alright, I'll guess I'll just wait for the bus and go back to London. I'm done. I can't find the way back myself. I'll just get caught again."

"Fine. Fuck you then."

She hung up, and I looked around my little home for the night – a crappy cut and copy bus shelter on the edge of a theme park at the arse end of London.

I try to lie down on the bench. Rain sprays in the wind and refreshes my face.

My phone buzzes.

COME BACK IN YOU LITTLE BITCH.

I am a little stung.

I text back:

OK. SEE YOU SHORTLY.

I take a breath, and set off.

I plunge into the undergrowth, picking my way between thorn bushes and dense copses, following some almost unseen half-forgotten path. I reach a wooden fence, and find a gap that has been torn open in the side by previous adventurers. I squeeze between broken, mouldering boards, avoiding the hang-nails, sweeping the leaves from my face. On the far side, the grasses grow up to my waist and the branches snag at my clothes as I push deeper and further. Boots sink into thick humus and drag through snarling ferns. I stumble and laugh and occasionally stop to sip consciously and cautiously from the wine bottle before pressing onwards. I am cautious to ration it, suddenly alone in the jungles of Greater Slough for who knows how long. The forest clears a little as the slopes rise upwards and roll down, and seemingly I am lost for moments in some vast jungle, heading further from civilisation and the beaten trail, deeper into the unknown.

After nearly an hour, I stumble suddenly back on to a road, and see the lights in the distance of the theme park's security gates. Here, I slip silently across the road to a chain link fence. A section of it has been collapsed and I step daintily over it and into the meadows beyond, keeping to the shadows of the sparse brush and trees beyond.

"Are there cows here?" I ask, a little concerned.

Now less than 50 metres from the security post with its floodlights and the park beyond. I stroll past the single wooden barrier, and into the park beyond. There is the derelict mock-up of the school bus, and I climb inside to contact the others, breathless and satisfied that I have made it back to the target alone.

They are not far, and after a few more texts I locate them, less than 50 metres away. I climb a small wall and drop down into a fake beach of sand, scrambling through the dunes, to find the rest of the cell huddled together inside a fake pirate ship.

"Hi everybody, sorry I'm late," I say as I scramble up.

"Oh my Gosh! Have you got wine left?"

I laugh, and climb into the pirate ship beside Mierda on the sand to share wine and huddle in the cold air, awaiting the opening of the park in the morning, where we can jump the queue for Oblivion and spend our day fishing food out of the bins, satisfied in the knowledge that I'd already had the greatest part of the thrill two times over.

I'd warned Pidge not to send him if he couldn't handle it.

"Tell him we're a bunch of sexy hobo alcoholic chaos punks and if he wants to live in a basement beneath that, he's totally welcome."

And still he came, flying from Berlin and spending a few hours trying to hitch from Stansted before giving up and taking the bus. We were upstairs, Mierda working in Shitty Tattoo Corner, when he popped in, looking like a young Gandalf, and was immediately rejected by Grizzly. He had a giggle like a slutty schoolgirl, with a bushy beard hanging to the middle of his chest, like a coil of wire wool. His eyes glittered like discs of MDMA crystal.

El Culo ended up staying a month, and would be our future gateway to the communes of Rigaerstrasse.

"How's it in Berlin?"

"I work two days a week selling beer to tourists in Mauer Park, and the rest of my time is spent looking for projects to get involved in."

"So how?"

"I was five years in the 'Metheuselah Mob' where we had no private possessions. I eventually left the community with a desire to hold on to many of the concepts and way of life that I had learnt during that time. I was squatting alone in Sydney initially, under a bridge."

"Like a troll."

"Too right. A damn stylish troll."

"So what's happening in your end then?"

"I'm in Rigaerstrasse for the radical left scene. The cops have declared it a 'danger zone'," and suddenly El Culo is singing at me, in a searing falsetto head back, beard resonating, pumping the air with a disco finger:

"HIGH-WAY-TO-THE-DANGER-ZONE!"

"Apparently a rock fell on a cop's car from some rooftop. Those buildings are very old. Hee hee hee."

I go out to check the little shop on Union Street to see if they will leave the bacon sandwiches out again, when he strolls up to me, tall and slim and black as the leather on my jacket, head topped by a 90s flat-top and an Adidas bag slung over one shoulder, strolling down from Elephant and Castle towards the London Bridge.

"Hey, hello, hi, I am just arrive here. I am looking for a place to stay. Maybe you know one hotel."

This isn't the first time I have been approached by people on the street looking for a squat or a place to stay, and I never really learned how to say no to such requests. I have learned to try and be careful, to try and be difficult, but often I just simply cannot say no to young people wandering the streets looking for a place to stay. I do my best to slow down the process, to get a feel for who this guy is.

"Yeah, er, maybe man. I'm just going to get some food. Maybe you want to come with me."

"Sure, ok I come with you. My name is Hanuc."

"George."

El Culo suddenly pops out of the crowd, giggling and smiling through his beard, and the three of us set off down to Union Street, talking idly.

"Yeah man, all the hotels here will be super expensive. There is the St Christopher's hostel just there that will be cheaper."

"Oh yeah I usually go there if I need beer and cigarettes, hee

hee hee," giggles El Culo.

Union Street is a bust, but during the walk we get to spend some time with Hanuc, and he seems harmless enough. I pull El Culo aside and whisper to him out of the corner of my mouth.

"What do you think?"

"He seems ok to me," he says. "But it's your house."

"Ugh," I sigh. "Property is theft right."

I pull up in front of Hanuc.

"So look man, maybe you can stay with us in the basement for a couple of days whilst you get yourself sorted. I'll tell the others that you are my friend and that you come to stay for a little while. OK?"

"Great, thanks man, that's great."

"Anarchy!" giggles El Culo, rummaging through a bin and pulling out some kebab meat in a styrofoam box.

"You say it in jest. But what's your take on it, Young Gandalf?" I ask.

El Culo pulls thoughtfully on his iron wool beard.

"Primarily, anarchy for me means total equality. It means the absence of the concept of property, as distinguishable from possession, and of course is marked by the absence of a police force, army, and organised gangs or militias. I believe that for anarchism to exist, it is necessary to have some kind of social or cultural basis for resistance to the accumulation of power and intolerance. That's why I find insurrectionary anarchism the most attractive and promising strand of anarchism. The idea being that groups of people committed to anarchist principles must resist being governed, but also foster alternative social structure and social spaces. The spread of anarchism in my opinion is best fostered by the open display of a 'better world'. I also believe money and the state to be inextricably linked, and believe that in a society devoid of the state, monetary exchanges would not be necessary or possible."

"What do you think Hanuc?"

"I have no idea what you talking about, man. I live in squats in Barcelona and I hear a lot about anarchy, it's crazy. I just happy I get a place to stay."

We take him to 101 and bang the door.

Bill opens it, totally naked, looking half asleep and a little drunk, his dick like a fist between his legs.

"This is Hanuc. He's going to stay for a few days."

Bill shrugs. "Come in. It's cold outside."

It would be 18 months before Hanuc finally left.

It's the week before Christmas. A sleazy rain is drizzling down on the Borough, the streets slick with puddles and vomit as squads of revellers tour between London Bridge and the Elephant. Mobs of people in gaudy Christmas jumpers, gold high-heels and elf hats mill in the road beside the Borough market, clasping wine glasses and pints of watery lager, faces locked in holiday rictus, whilst clumsy wailing teenage girls dodge between the slow slurry of traffic painted in sinister yellows by the streetlights. The pavements are packed, and I slip between over-flowing bins of kebab meat and discarded bottles and the club-footed staggerings of men in suits holding the arms of cackling women as they make their way to the office parties. Flashes of Fairytale of New York, Last Christmas, Wizzard, spill from the doorways of venues rammed with jigging bodies flailing their limbs in the air, seemingly packed against the glass of the building like too many monkeys in the zoo. Dour-faced security in rain jackets mirthlessly search bags and answer slurred questions. Each metre seems packed with potential danger, and moving my way through the crowd feels like eating birthday cake off a landmine – a good time in a dystopia.

Over the road, I slip past the statue of the charging soldier outside the Slug and Lettuce, the outline of his perpetual assault haloed in neon blue by the pub's signage. Skipping a puddle, I glide between a double-decker bus that parps its horn petulantly at me and a dark-tinted Mercedes that pulses with sullen anonymous bass.

Another 100 metres of weaving lurching, shell-shocked pedestrians and I am at the door of 101.

There is someone near comatose on the doorstep, head slumped between their knees, long blonde bangs hanging almost to the pavement. I ignore them, and bang the reassuring wood.

Moments later, Pinky opens the door, smiling coyly, a vision in pink with matching elf hat, and she lets me inside.

A dozen or so people are engaged in some riotous debate inside: El Culo pulling his long wizard's beard and giggling like a toy machine gun; Bill rattles off some extended monologue on the virtues of Fela Kuti's polygamous house of amazon wives and guerrilla musicians, singing muses and soldiers with bass guitars; Nieszka sits whispering earnestly in the ear of Fyodor, whose head is lolling in steady circles and his low Vostok tones mumbling near incoherently, cut by bursts of rapid laughter; Awi stood hopping from foot to foot, gabbling. Everyone seems to be talking at once, and bottles of whisky and gin and vodka and wine and beer are circling around the low table like flies circling a corpse.

The door slams behind me, sealing out one madness and locking me in with another. I move hesitantly forward. From the basement below I hear the rattle-crash-bang of drums and the soaring thrum of distorted bass. Daigas and Ona the Feral are playing kicker on the little table El Culo rebuilt after finding it in a bin. I move towards a chair, when I see Mierda hovering by the stairs, fixing me with those lead eyes.

She says it softly, matter of factly, so that only I can hear it over the tumult around us.

"Bezdalius is dead."

"What?"

She doesn't say anything else. She turns and heads up the stairs, leaving me to stand, ignored and uncomprehending, processing this new information, trying to rework my perception of reality, and most of all, figure out how to respond.

After a moment, I follow her up the three flights of winding stairs, gripping the bannister all the way up, thoughts cold and numb.

I step through our doorway, treading carefully over boards laid over the naked floor, dodging the holes and finding her sitting in a chair in the room, alone.

I sit opposite her.

"So what happened?"

"They found him. He hung himself. Six months ago. They found him hanging in Alpha House, one of the buildings we used to squat. He'd been there about two weeks already, back in July. His ex-girlfriend just found him in one of the morgues. No one knew who he was."

There are tears in her eyes. I realise I have never seen Mierda cry before.

"I knew. I knew already. I knew that either he was crazy insane somewhere or that he had fucking killed himself. That's why I did this."

She shows me the tattoo she had been carving into her ankle, working on it since we were in Dock Street: a cartoon poop, the dripping fluid from which spells out the words RIP.

She looks at me again, and very softly, almost inaudibly, she says:

"I need you."

I take her in my arms. It is awkward and uncomfortable, like holding a wooden marionette, but I persist. I persist because I do not know what else to do.

"I don't want to be used anymore."

Whilst I hold her, I cannot help but picture Bezdalius climbing into the empty building. He would have been taking huge amounts of speed for days, if not weeks. He would have prepared his best outfit, spiked and coloured his hair to perfection, a halo crown of multicoloured spikes. Wearing Christmas socks, no doubt. He would have left no note. He would have prepared the rope, and chosen a spot somewhere central. I see him pulling a chair over, and throwing the rope over the girder. Methodical, cold, calculated, I see him secure the rope, and ceremonially fit the noose around his neck. He probably practised tying and untying it secretly for weeks before, making sure it was perfect. He tightens the noose, stands on the chair and pauses, just a moment, to consider.

Then, he kicks the chair away.

I hope it snapped his neck. But I see him swinging and dancing, hands clutching at the rope as it chokes him, face turning red, then purple, then black as it squeezes the life out of him. It begins to spin as he swings and spasms and dances on the end. No way back. Finally, he shits himself, and cums, and pisses himself, all at once – the grand finale.

He hangs there, festering, for two weeks, unbothered by flies, until somebody finds him. He would have hoped it was a landlord or a cop, that would never, ever forget the image or the smell.

"Naiad said he was the first one to go of all of us."

"Fucking suicide squad."

"It was when I was away. Maybe if I had been here I could have helped him. He was like my twin brother, you know. Like I could read his thoughts."

I release her, and she wipes angrily at the tears that have appeared mysteriously on the mask of her face.

"I need a fucking drink."

So we drink, and we drink, and we drink.

The party-funeral-wake rages downstairs, and people lurch between manic celebration and sour reminiscence, swapping stories of Bezdalius and talking utter, utter shit, the gabbling havoc of a Hogarth gin-orgy.

"One time he stole a cross from outside a church -"

"-he performed in Barcelona dressed as a giant comic-book Mariachi with cardboard guitar and sombrero -"

"- when he broke his back falling off that building -"

"- when he climbed to the top of Millennium Mills -"

"- dead the cunt fucking dead dead dead -"

"- left a message on the fridge in Squatopolis, said 'rot in pieces'-"

"- stole me a hundred quid's worth of paintbrushes -"

"- kept his speed in a guitar pedal -"

"- loaded a suitcase full of tools in B&Q and walked right out -"

"- arrested for wearing a Maddy t-shirt that said: 'dead girls don't cry'-"

"- stop and searched by cops who asked him what it was for-"

"- cracked a building with a ninja crowbar -"

"- I knew -"

"- when they asked if he played guitar, he said 'no'-"

"- fucking cunt -"

"Dead."

"All of us."

It swirls on and on. Later, I find Mierda on the stairs, leaning in a corner, wiping tears from her eyes, and I try to comfort her.

She pushes me back. "Can you just fuck me?"

I pull down her shorts and she pulls open my trousers, but my dick is like a piece of rope, and we fumble drunkenly and incoherently against each other before realising it is useless. We pull our clothes back up and drag each other up the stairs to our mattress to collapse and ignore this terrible reality.

They are leaving for La Jungla – a long-weekend party of booze, drugs, grind core and rave at an old squat in Barcelona. Mierda and Naiad and a selection of the others, buzzing around packing their bags and cackling excitedly at their approaching debauch. I am drunk, I know, and trying to think about my own trip with

Pidge – a month in Southeast Asia, hitch-hiking and roaming, back to the tropics after a long absence. It has been arranged for months. I would give anything not to be going.

I feel hollow and sad, like the holiday season has autopsied me whilst I am still alive, begun pickling my system and preserving my various organs in mason jars around me. There is a large scab on my head from New Year's Eve from where the youths smashed a bottle of whisky over my head at the Canning Town rave. I have yet to pack my own bags, despite my flight being only a day after theirs. I wish I was going with them. I don't feel great about being separated from my crew. I want to just drag Mierda back to the little nest we have shared on the top floor this last few months. The little nest she always teases me about sneaking my way into, claiming there were no rooms left in the house, the little nest I blagged my way into by saying "oh, I'm leaving next week" and "oh, I won't be here all the time".

"I never lived with a male before. I always kicked them out."

I have been around everyone in the house, collecting music on my hard-drive, asking them to give me a selection of their own choice. Nieszka gives solemn, gothic deutsche-trance and breakcore. Bill gives everything from southern Gospel jazz to nu-school hip-hop crunk and afrobeat madness. Mierda, a selection of power violence, mash-up noise-punk, twisted Oi piss-takes and shitcore. There is even Bezdalius' seminal "Man Is The Bored" creation – a dozen acapella grind core songs, performed by pounding a pen and a hand on a desk whilst going "duh-duh-duh-duh" with your mouth. Classics all. I distract myself sitting alone in the front room, flicking through the files. It feels good to be taking pieces of them with me.

I don't know what I will come back to. Giles always said that it would be around the new year that he would want his building back, and it seems likely that I will walk out from building 101 and never return. I torture myself with visions of Mierda in our room, Mierda drunk and on speed in Barcelona, Mierda pursued by hungry punks with dreadlocked mullets.

Grizzly is stressed too, and lurks on the first staircase landing, head tucked under her tail, eyes querulous and uncertain at what is happening. I approach her too drunkenly, too openly, to try and comfort her, and she snaps out at my hand, not breaking the skin but giving me a clear warning to fuck right off. I tear a little at the rejection.

Finally, around midnight, the time comes. Naiad and Mierda are whirling out through the door.

Mierda wraps her arms around me and plants a chaste kiss on my cheek.

"I'm terrible at goodbyes, and hellos, and everything. I'll see you in a month. Have fun in Southeast Asia. Don't fuck too many ladyboys."

I smile as well as I can, and hug her, and kiss her cheek, and then she is saying good-bye to Grizzly, who looks more heart-broken than I feel, and then she is gone, the door slams behind her, and they are gone.

I sit on the stairs, and cry. What a fucking year it has been.

Awi and Hanuc stand awkwardly around me.

"Dude – it's only for a month."

BABIES
MACHT
FREI

Dear groups, individuals and collectives,

"Es ist besser unsere Jugend besetzt leere Häuser als fremde Länder" (In our youth it is better to squat empty houses than foreign countries).

Under this motto some young people started squatting houses in Rigaerstrasse and in the rest of Friedrichshain in the early 90s, creating places where they could collectively live, organise and resist.

Particularly in the following years many of the squatted houses were evicted or pressed to sign contracts as a result of the so called "Berliner Line" (Berliner Linie) which aimed to push people into a capitalistic (consumptive) lifestyle. Even the contracts didn't prevent houses getting evicted in many cases. Nevertheless a few of the originally squatted houses persist as active spaces.

Discounting these projects that have remained, with somewhat affordable rent – the rest of our Kiez has undergone drastic changes in rent costs and real estate prices that are obvious to see / hard to ignore, with formidable and unaffordable prices for flats.

These changes have squeezed out not only the people living in house projects, but also people whose families have lived here in Friedrichshain for centuries, subsequently forcing them to leave their homes and move to the outskirts of the city. But all of this won't happen without us throwing a spanner in the cogs of the capitalist machine so driven by the logic of exploitation. So we take our resistance to the current situation to the streets.

Resistance to the exclusion of collective living and project spaces has been happening since the first houses were squatted.

For this reason we invite you to join us in celebrating 25 years of resistance and self-organisation in and around Rigaerstrasse from the 06.07 to 12.07. During this week workshops, presentations, an alley cat race, concerts, exhibitions, actions, discussions will all take place (as well as anything else you have in mind).

Films will also be screened during the week as part of a Film Festival. On Wednesday 8th of July a free flea market is planned (an exhibition of money-less exchange).

We want to make this without any interference or input from institutions which would naturally dictate to us the direction and conditions of our event, but of course not without you. If you would like to participate in the free flea market or to have an information stand, to make a presentation, workshop, coffee or cake etc we'd be happy to hear from you. Or if you'd just like to drop by and check it out.

With the street festival we want to make a stand against the politics of gentrification in our neighbourhood (kiez). It is really important for us that the focus is on political content and community – collective exchange between people, we are not interested in making an event just for drinking without any content of substance.

So if you would like to come and join us in celebrating the 25 year anniversary of the projects in and around Rigaerstrasse!"

Call-out from the organisers

9

On the Edge of a Nervous System

We're not feeling edgy – the system is feeling nervous.
Red Army Faktion

Rigaerstrasse runs like a crowbar through the East Berlin kiez of Friedrichshain, curling at the ends at Frankfurter Allee railway station in the East and Besarinplatz in the West. It is the frontline trench of the gentrification war that has taken place on these streets for a quarter of a century now. Down one side, rows of mid-rise apartments, glistening freshly painted white, with skeletal frames of scaffold growing up the side and young mothers rolling their children to and fro. The graffiti at the bottom grows back like brightly coloured mould, with seemingly daily attempts to cleanse and purge it, a living struggle between some kind of organic growth and a perseverant nurse trying to expunge it. Black-clad military *polizei* – their faces like corrupted metal kettles left too long in the rain – lurk in ominous groups in doorways, some of them with large Auschwitzhunds on chains.

Down the other side, the communes of Rigaerstrasse: XB-liebig, R94, the punk bars of Abstand and Fischladen. Here, the rebellious fungus has successfully consumed the buildings, drowning them in ever changing and mutating layers of colour and rage. Thick layers of curling gig posters and fliers coil up off the walls like scales of armour. Punks and leftists patrol and laze outside the various doorways, watching the *polizei* watching them watching them. Many are drinking casually. Banners and flags fly from the windows, fluttering in the soft summer breeze, proclaiming defiance and solidarity: R94 BLEIBT!; SOLIDARITY WITH HAMBI!

We park down the road, near to the wagenplatz that sits near the Besarinplatz end, and stroll down Rigaerstrasse in the mid-morning sun. Down seemingly every road to each side, we spot the huge armoured trucks of the *polizei,* often loaded with a cargo of miserable and sinister looking cops who peer hatefully at us through the windows.

At R94, the double-doors are guarded by a smiling man with a blonde mohawk and eyes pale as a summer sunset. He welcomes us through, never taking his eyes off the squad of cops opposite.

"El Culo? Ja, he might be inside somewhere. Stay in the yard and someone will let you in."

We step through the short corridor into the cool interior of R94 with two doors, one directly to the left and the other opposite us. Various bicycles and tables are set up, expectantly, and a number of large bins yawn open, suspiciously empty. The yard is cool and sheltered, again the walls a mixture of decades old layers of graffiti, and freshly reclaimed and repainted works to the other side. Even here, this close to the source, the pressures of gentrification are creeping in.

Someone opens the side door, and me, Mierda, Grizzly, Naiad, Barnabas and Fyodor slip through, sneaking in past the thick, medieval barricades of stanchion posts and cages and portcullis, through some small rooms decorated with anarchic disregard for uniformity, and into Katerschmiede.

El Culo is playing chess at the bar, stood up, stroking his long wizard beard and smoking a cigarette. He looks up as we enter, smiling and giggling with that twinkle of mischief in his eye, bounding over to wrap long welcoming arms around each of us, immediately talking ten to the dozen.

"Ah! You're finally here! You're a bit late. You missed the *polizei* coming around and stealing all our trash. We were having a street-market on the first day and they raided it and forced everyone inside. They raided the children's creche as well. Forced all of them inside too. But then they came back and they took away all our rubbish. Said it was a potential weapon, hee

hee hee."

"How's it been going?"

"Yeah, really great. Later on the original squatters from when they occupied this building are going to come along and meet everyone. You should meet them too. I imagine for them it was a bit more like how London is now. And I'll be doing some movie screenings. I'm programming the whole week of cinema. Here tonight, and then some other places along the strasse over the week. So you guys live here now, right? Hee hee hee. Here, you want a beer? They make it locally here, look at the name: 1312. Hee hee hee. You play chess?"

And so on it goes. El Culo is expansive and welcoming, giving us all the graces, and after a few beers in Katerschmiede he tours us through to the second courtyard, this one full of trees and dogs and punks, with a home-made stage and seating laid out for some theatre.

"So this is where you'll be performing George. Everyone's very excited. Hee hee hee."

We loop around, climbing up the innards of the mid-rise through the high, spacious stairwells so common in Berlin. Landing after landing is drenched in posters for gigs and actions, the walls tagged and re-tagged with Left propaganda and punk humour.

"So most of the floors of the housing project pay some kind of rent, but there are a few spaces that are still squatted," El Culo explains as we loop up to the third floor. He pauses at a bricked-up doorway. "This was the old punk kitchen, but it got so bad that when everyone went out one day they just bricked it up. Hee hee hee."

He guides us through immaculate kitchens with polished hardwood floor and meticulously organised shelves of utensils, pans, spices, healthy-looking plants and orderly recycling points of paper, plastic and glass. In his kitchen, he points out his pride and joy.

"Look, we built our own cinema, and run it off a cherry pie."

He folds down a huge, pristine canvas from the ceiling that fills the central space of the kitchen.

"We spend a lot of time here, hee hee hee."

We weave through some more corridors. Everything is connected in a circular way, leading between the two stairwells, and the effect is disorientating.

We find our way to the guestroom – past some small spaces filled with furniture and chaos – painted pale green with tall, bright windows looking out over the leafy green courtyards. Nieszka is here, smiling broadly and welcoming us with little chaste hugs. She doesn't like to be touched.

Here, El Culo turns to us with officious severity.

"So if you hear an air-raid siren, that means the police are trying to break-in. You're here as my guests so it's best for you to find me, or to gather in Katerschmiede downstairs and some people will explain what is going on. It's quite unlikely, but it has happened before, that they want to come in and have a look around. Generally we tell them no. They have to be pretty committed to want to come all the way in here. Hee hee hee. So we have various plans which because of security culture I can't tell you here. You should assume that the whole building is bugged and that anything you say is being recorded. This whole area has been termed a 'danger zone' since a large piece of stone fell off the roof and it nearly hit a cop car. I think it's just because we can't afford repairs on the roof. Hee hee hee. Oh yes, you should see the roof. The roof is nice. Excellent vantage point. Hee hee hee."

We climb up some more stairs, finding a ladder going up to the roof through a trapdoor already open, and we climb up, working together to clumsily lift Grizzly up through the hole and on to the roof.

It is vast, and Friedrichshain spreads out around us, a factory forest of mid-rise apartments. Here, the graffiti mould rolls in waves over the short walls that divide the house and over the very roof itself. We stroll to the edge and peer off, looking down at a polizeiwagen rolling down the street towards Besarinplatz.

"Just down there is Silvio-Meier Strasse," explains El Culo. "He was an antifascist killed in Samariterstrasse. They renamed the street after him."

The wind is cool up here, the skies above blue and cloudless, Berlin stretching out before us like a jungle of opportunity. We smile, and laugh, and open the bottles of beer El Culo had forced into our hands, forgetting to ask for any money. We toast our arrival, and to the Long Week ahead, celebrating 25 years of the Rigaerstrasse Commune.

We settle into a Long Week in Rigaerstrasse, rising late for a lunch of *brotchen* and *weissalad* from the REWE, lifting a packet of one of the dozens of incredible herbal teas they champion in Germany, drinking it down with morning coffees and then spending slow afternoons patrolling between XB-Liebig and Fischladen. We collect empty bottles of beer rigorously and turn them in at the spety to get cents off our next bottles of Sterny.

"It's like society is divided into those who leave the bottles, and those who collect them," muses Mierda as we clink more abandoned treasure-trash into our cloth bag to take away.

The house projects were originally squatted and defended from eviction with the kind of militant vigour you would expect from ex-Soviet bloc youth. The same kind of vigour that celebrates Walpurgisnacht every year with burning cars and street warfare as a celebration of anti-capitalism. El Culo is less sure.

"It's just become a training exercise for the cops," he explains. "Once a year they get a big opportunity to try out all their new equipment and tactics. They love the water cannons here."

"BoJo bought some broken ass ex-Irish ones after the 2011 riots, but they've never been deployed in the mainland UK. I was in Malaysia before at a big demo where they had them. We had a giant monster puppet parading and playing in the street, and the water cannons took it as target practice. Blasted it to pieces."

"They can take people's faces off," adds in Mierda, a little distantly. We all pause over our beers to muse at the idea of having the very skin and flesh flayed from our faces in the name of public order.

Everyday, the house projects take turns to host a *kufa* – formally known as *voku*, or people's kitchen – but changed after a Berlin-wide plenum of the squats decided that the latter was too politically incorrect. The same kind of plenum changed the famous "no justice, no peace, fuck the police" chant to something else by majority vote.

Each day, we drift down to one of the projects to provide a donation for pizza, brown rice, tofu and shaitan, beans and chili, potato salads, all made vegan and shockingly delicious. As the evenings close in, the houses host electronic noise, punk and hardcore bands. Fyodor is in heaven, skipping from one band to the next, grooving off the drums and the noise, excitedly enjoying his holiday until he is so drunk he is slurring his words and laughing and wobbling through the streets as if concussed.

Naiad and Barnabas seem more distant, sleeping in the van and complaining.

"What do you want to do here? It's boring," moans Naiad.

Mierda is incensed: "There's a whole festival on! Why not get involved and try talking to some people?"

They head off to the centre instead, visiting museums and parks whilst we drink and borracho in the streets like filthy punks.

One day, they hold a zinemarket in the courtyard at R94, and Mierda brings out copies of *Il Manual di Clitoride,* attempting the same tactic that worked so well at Crack!Fest. She approaches a table staffed by two females with severe Berlin haircuts, rings through their noses, and the Teutonic disdain for charm. Their patches are of vaginas in white-relief on black, held open by a finger, or cartoonish tampons blooded at one end like totemic talismans.

"Maybe you want to swap? I have this manual here all about the clitoris, so if your boyfriend is useless -"

"I don't have a boyfriend," snaps one of the table-staffers, with contemptuous condescension. Mierda is a little shaken, and wobbles off from the table with a sad little frown on her face, lip stuck out and pouting in mock upset.

"Don't worry, Mierda," I tell her. "In Germany, they call that making friends."

We browse through the free-zine tables, loading up with photostatted, handmade booklets on the Conspiracy of the Cells of Fire in Greece, on lists of actions against banks, ATMs, police cars and mobile phone masts made by the ELF and Tendency Towards The Wild in Mexico. There is a table from Rozbrat, a squat in Poland, and I approach one with a copy of my book, giving the usual *spiel* about exchange and barter. A young Pole with dreadlocks and a weasel face takes it and says he isn't sure.

"We have to make our money back for the squat," he explains. "Not all of this is for us, you see. I have to speak with the others."

I raise my hands in supplication. "Sure, sure, sure, have a talk with the others, have a look at the book, if you decide you want to swap, then that would be great. If not, no problem. I understand. *Capitalismus*!"

I watch him from the other side of the yard, and see him getting drawn into the book as he leafs through it. He speaks to some of the others, and I see stern matrons placing their hands on their hips and frowning.

After some moments, he comes over with a little pile of patches, zines and a t-shirt.

"We would like to offer this!" he says.

"That's wonderful," I reply. "But is it ok if I take a different t-shirt?"

The courtyard at the housing project in Friedrichshain is cool and sunny, trees and bushes growing calmly between the four walls, decked with the ubiquitous motifs of Berlin – graffiti tags and street-art murals, stencils and sloganeering that quickly becomes an agitative wallpaper to the autonomous spaces of Berlin. On benches and stools amidst the foliage, a few earnest looking activist types, peaceably smiling hippies and our motley crew of alcohol-doused travellers is assembled, sipping Sternies and awkwardly eyeing each other as we try to anticipate which way the next hour of our lives is going to go.

Two of the organisers are squabbling in the manner of people to whom organisation is something extremely important yet slightly mystifying as a process, something akin to quantum physics or finer points of religious dogma. Sounding like they are extremely annoyed with each other, they are actually just earnestly working out what order things should go in.

We are gathered in a circle around a sheet laid on the cobbles of the floor. It is littered with a heap of DIY pleasure devices: dildoes and ticklers and weird, nobbled contraptions, made from inner tubes and bike parts and recycled materials. They are intriguingly odd and mysterious, somehow unreachable and distant, yet so familiar and tantalising – kitsch mementos from a saucy postcard holiday in a scrapyard. I cannot help but cast an eye-round at the assembled persons, and picturing them engaging with each device, the placid polite demeanour of their faces shattered by orgasmic self-pleasuring. I admit, I was open to explore some possibilities.

"Hello, and *wilkommen,* thank you for coming to our workshop on masturbation. We have organised this workshop because we feel it relates to something that is still taboo in our culture. Something connected with our ideas of sexuality, both public and private, and how this relates to our gender-normative behaviours towards one another.

"To begin with, let's begin by getting suggestions on

euphemisms we use to talk about masturbation. Can anyone make a suggestion for another word we use to describe the act of self-love?"

There is an awkward silence. The facilitators use this natural pause for thought to produce a piece of A3 paper and a marker pen which they snap the lid off of with some noticeable satisfaction, before returning to look at us all with po-faced expectation.

"You mean, apart from 'self-love'?"

"Yes – something else."

Some bold activist type in a Buzzcocks tee-shirt raises his hand.

"Yes?"

"Err...choking the chicken."

Some people can't help but smile, uncertain of whether it's appropriate or not. The facilitator studiously writes "choking the chicken" on the piece of paper in neat bold letters.

"Yes. Good. Any more."

Another extended pause. People are bearing their teeth at each other in half-leers, half-rictus terror and bemusement.

"Spanking the monkey."

Giggles.

"*Funf gegen Willy, bis Willy kotzt.*"

"Five against Willy, until Willy pukes."

Cackles now, people can't hold it anymore.

"Ah, yes, good."

Scribble scribble goes the stone-faced facilitator, as people snigger and smirk.

"*Drenar la vena principal, en espano*l."

"Drain the main vein."

"Ah, good, yes."

"Shaking white hot coconuts from the veiny love tree."

"Er – wait, could you repeat that?"

"Shake hands with the unemployed."

"*Jouer avec le baguette magique.*"

"*Bić niemca.*"

"What's that?"

"It's Polish…It means to 'punch a German'."

People are openly laughing now, apart from the facilitator with the pen, who is furiously documenting this important cultural research.

"So, looking at this list, do you notice anything about the examples we have here?"

Suddenly serious and studious, the assembled lean in and peruse over the list with the gravity of scholars.

"Well, several of them sound quite violent."

"Especially towards animals."

"And Germans."

"Good, yes. This relates to our perceptions of masturbation being something shameful, hidden, even violent. A self-violence. This highlights the subliminal relationship between sex and power."

The facilitator with the pen has finally caught up and lifts her head to join in. "In many cultures masturbation is seen as a failure, as self-abusing even. There are many myths around the damage masturbation can do to a person."

"That you go blind. Or grow hairs on the palms."

"Yes. Like you would become a mutant for touching yourself. A werewolf even. It starts from a very early age, when young children become aware of the sensitivity of their sexual organs, and begin to play with themselves, touch themselves, in a very innocent way, in public or in front of others. And then they are told "No! That is bad! That is wrong! You should not touch yourself like that!"

"It is one of the first traumas inflicted on us by adults."

"So what, are you advocating that we let children play with themselves in public? And adults too?"

"We are saying that there might be other ways to address sexual behaviour that avoids shaming people about masturbation."

"Are you saying that we should be able to masturbate in public?"

"That would be an interesting direct action."

"We will talk more about this later. But also I have some questions for you. When you masturbate, are you very loud? Do you make as much noise when you masturbate as when you are with another person?"

People think.

"I guess I feel that part of the noises I make during sex are to encourage and communicate with the other person there."

"Yes, but then why not make these noises for ourselves when we are masturbating? Why not encourage and communicate with ourselves when engaging in self-love?"

"Yes," says the facilitator with the pen with lively enthusiasm. "When I masturbate people can hear it all through the house. I make a point of being actively vocal and allowing myself the release – not to be ashamed. People still laugh when I come out of the bathroom alone, they wonder where the other person is! But why shouldn't I fuck myself – loudly and proudly – as passionately as I fuck other people?"

The image and the question hang in the air as people picture what it must be like to live with this person, or indeed, with a household of proudly vocal wankers.

"What else do you notice about this list?"

"It's all for male masturbation."

"That's right. Even in a circle like this, we can see the patriarchal domination of our sexuality. If male masturbation is taboo, then female masturbation does not even exist."

She pauses for dramatic effect.

The marker pen lid clicks off again.

"So, can we now make a list of euphemisms for female masturbation, or more gender-neutral terms?"

This allows people to relax. After a moment's thought, the suggestions start to come thick and fast.

"Feeding the pony."

"Double-clicking the mouse."

"Flicking the bean."

"Provoking the little man in the boat."

"Menage a moi."

"Paddling the pink canoe."

"DIY time."

"Butterin' your muffin."

Diligently, the facilitator continues to scribble down every utterance as the group descends into equal parts clinical professionality and exuberant laughter.

We proceed to hand out the toys and pass around the manuals on sexual positions and the positive benefits of onanism, but the vibe of an Anne Summers party held in a suburban housewives front room for the itinerant members of a breakaway Women's Institute faction is unnervingly hard to shake off. My friends are growing restless with this process. One of them cannot contain themselves any longer. Leaping to their feet, they cry out:

"Surely we have had enough of the theory, when will the practical begin?"

"But wait we still have some points on the agenda of the workshop -"

Silence. The interlocuter pushes forward.

"Fuck the agenda! Are we just going to sit around talking about it, or are we going to start wanking?"

"Yes! Finally. This is the real reason we are all here. So why are we jerking each other off with all this theory? Let's get down to it?"

"Ok – let's stop beating around the bush and beat our own bushes."

Enthusiastic wavy hands in the air from all around the circle. There is that frozen moment, which William Burroughs referred to as "the naked lunch" – that moment when you see what is on the end of everyone's forks. Over the next 20 minutes or so, I can recall three such moments. The first, once everyone in that circle had begun manipulating themselves, hands inside their jeans or openly displaying their junk to the circle, that wild mania in their eyes, the crazed disbelief that they had finally started *to do something*.

The second, about halfway in, as people began to writhe and moan and twist their faces in that lascivious mutant manner of the sexually-possessed, the girl who favoured vocal self-encouragement wailing like a banshee, leading us all in a cat-calling cacophony of joyous ecstatic shouting, shrieking and gasping. I suspect someone wandered in at this point before promptly turning around and exiting.

And the final, as one by one we died out, wanking ourselves to satisfaction and relaxing, rosy-cheeked and sticky-handed and bright-eyed staring at each in wonderment at how fucking radical and free we all were.

And then, silence.

"So…how was the workshop?"

"Shall we make some action points on what to do next?"

"Hmm. Maybe now we can all take turns fucking each other?"

"Or just keep on fucking ourselves? Shall we put it to the vote?"

As evening sets over the mid-rises of Friedrichshain, the sun splashing the multicoloured walls with tones of copper and gold, we gather en masse in the crossroads between Rigaer and Liebigstrasse, hundreds of Berlin's youth and old guard: leather-bound punks with band advertisements plastered across them, llama-wool clad hippies in Aladdin pants, terse *activisten* with suspicious backpacks and sharp-eyes, rolling merry drunks supping Sternbergers and half-dancing across the street and the whole gamut of the ultraleft and affiliates. We sit in the streets, drinking with impunity, or stand admiring the sun as it blasts across the front of XB-Liebig. There is to be a march, a demonstration of our solidarity and defiance. There are many, many *polizeiwagens* parked in both directions, lurking, trying to remain inconspicuous, like a pride of giant metal lions surrounding a herd of limber gazelles. The shops around us have pulled down their shutters in expectation.

We are looking up towards XB-Liebig, and from one of the upstairs windows, someone has placed an amplifier, and a young female with cropped blonde hair and an unsteady voice takes up a microphone to make a speech to the assembled mob.

El Culo makes a rambling translation:

"Er...gathered in spirit of defiance, solidarity. Reclaiming our streets. Reclaiming our *kiez*. We remember 25 *jahres* of resistance against unaffordable rents. Expulsion of families that have lived here for centuries. Take it to the streets to throw a spanner in the works of capitalism. You know the kind of thing."

The speech goes on longer, and then, the climax. Masked figures on the roof of XB-Liebig ignite coloured smoke bombs, and a tremendous roar goes up from the crowd as the sound system in the window starts blasting *La Rage,* by Kenny Arkana. El Culo giggles.

"That's the signal, everybody stay close."

Seemingly with a mind of its own, the crowd begins to move, rolling like an unsteady fog down Liebigstrasse towards the dual avenue of Samariterstrasse. We are hundreds strong, many clad in black and masked already. It is only as we begin to move that I realise something.

"Shit," I say to Mierda. "I'm still wearing my Crocs."

"Oh George," she laughs. "Going to riot in Crocs? You absolute hipster."

It is too late to change. We are on the move.

Cries of *anti-capitalista, antifascista,* of no justice, no peace, fight the police roll through the crowd with cheers and calls of ACAB. People are clapping and blowing whistles, and with glacial momentum we surge down the hill and out into the broad avenues of Samariterstrasse. Collectively, we begin to march, and for a time as I stumble up and down the middle of the roads in my Crocs, we run the streets. We march clear and strong, me and Mierda linking arms.

Yet as it grows darker and darker, the whole street seems to turn black-and-blue. The flashing lights of the *polizei* illuminate both ends of the avenue. The *polizeiwagen*s that had lurked in the sidelines now pull into the main road, blocking both ends. The march slows, stops, people looking in both directions. Some bottles fly overhead, the sound of breaking glass. There are screams in the crowd, sounds of panic and attack, brief skirmishes breaking out between towering armoured shadows and apes that seem naked by contrast. I can see these huge, grotesque rhinocerosmen stabbing their fists into screaming shapes ahead of us. The blue lights flash off their armour. Behind us, more screams, panic, the sound of Germanic, authoritarian voices over loudspeakers. The looming shapes of the armoured cars, metal mesh pulled down over the windshields. The crowd is nervous, circling back and forth. More screams and panic. We see a young woman on the floor, people trying to carry her, others trying to pull her back, and for a moment she is caught in a tormented rack-stretch between anonymous shapes in black.

I stumble and scuff my feet, bouncing through a few people. I have lost Mierda, Naiad, Barnabas, everyone, in the foaming sea of people mulling around the avenue. I lose a Croc in some broken glass, find it again, and stagger on.

Ahead, I can see the line of police closing the street. There are intermittent shouts of "*Fight the police*!" echoing around, punctuated by siren calls and the droning, robotic chatter of the loudspeakers.

I find Mierda, holding Grizzly on the leash, and grab on to her arm.

"Yeah, me in Crocs, you walking a dog through a riot." I laugh.

"They grabbed that girl. She wasn't even doing anything," she is saying. "They properly fucked her up."

I take her by the arm and we begin to cut through the crowd, heading towards the sideroads, left open for exactly this purpose. Trapped on the main roads, the options are limited: direct confrontation with the police, or disperse down the alleys into the *kiez*. More rocks and bottles are flying, and there are angry roars from sections of the crowd. We are not the first to begin to look for a way out.

We scurry across broken glass and through the packs of police skirmishing the fringes of the mob. Already many people have departed, finding the situation futile. We head down Silvio-Meier-Strasse, and turn sharply, heading back to R94.

At the door of R94, someone has helpfully piled dozens of cobblestones, pulled from the pavements and roads all around Friedrichshain. A figure in a black mask with pale blue eyes stands by the door, systematically picking each rock and with expert practice flinging it at the *polizeiwagens* that pass by, or that are parked over the road. One by one, the little stones fly off into the darkness, and occasionally we hear them smack satisfyingly against metal, glass or kevlar.

The barricade swings closed behind us, sealing out the sound of riot, and in the sudden tomblike calm we can hear only our ragged breathing.

10

Mother Black Cunt's Revenge

> *The coming communities are more likely to be found in those crucibles of human sociability and creativity out of which the radically new emerges: racialized and ethnicized identities, queer and youth subcultures, anarchists, feminists, hippies, indigenous peoples, back-to-the-landers, "deviants" of all kinds in all kinds of spaces.*
> Richard J.F. Day, Gramschi is Dead: Anarchist Currents in the Newest Social Movements

"So, are you lot a bunch of anarchists then?"

A lost soul, abandoned by the Thursday night Camden carnival, meandered out of the desolate early morning wasteland that lies between Koko on Mornington Crescent and the Roundhouse at Chalk Farm. He wandered up to us in the hope of some after-hours entertainment, a disciple of the depressive hedonist coda that states that any and all persons must be available to amuse and bemuse at all hours. The six of us stand clutching a guilty bag of tools and locks at the junction of Kentish Town Road and Camden High Street, midway through our planning meeting, eyeing the target opposite us. As I stare through him, with his earnest, ovine eyes and blank hopeful expression, I feel a rising clot of disgust congeal within me. Here was one of the enemy, or at best one of those gradually trampling the identity and difference of the Borough into the ground. A man-child of the millennium, a fecund and facile consumer-construct, choking the world with his insipidity, asphyxiating through mediocrity.

He stands directly between us and the gloomy husk of the Black Cunt – boarded with black hoardings the night before – the gold lettering painted across the front glittering faintly in the sterile light of a double-decker night bus grumbling south. Its owners, Kicking Horse Limited, gave the staff 24-hours' notice and closed the venue, ambushing the shocked and indignant crowds with the announcement on her ultimate night. Their plan, as with all property developers, is to create new avenues for the affluent gentry, to penetrate the remnants of autonomous culture struggling on in London.

I look around our group of six – the *KRÜ KRU* angry fuck brigade in full war regalia – tight denim and ragged leather splattered with patches reading "fuck the system", "fashion is my philosophy", "mutants"; belts of metal studs, Mercedes Benz trophies and bullets; faux animal skin prints of leopard, zebra, jaguar; ripped fishnet stockings pouring from cut-off jeans hot pants; hair in knotty tentacles of dreadlocks, sides shaved to the skin, painted emerald, azure, purple, black, strung with ornaments of severed dolls' heads and mystic street totems; tattoos of rats and sea witches, Russian dolls with balaclavas and Virgin Marys holding crowbars; dramatic eye make-up and silver piercings through lips, septa, tongues; black boots and fingerless gloves. Most would assume we are part of the children's crusade that marches up and down Camden High Street every weekend – yet another crew of hopeless fashionistas concocting an identity through accessories, victims of manufactured desires and programmed insecurities. If anything, we were the antithesis of a black bloc – anonymous in our extreme individuation – at least, from an external point of view. Yet I'd bet almost none of the zombified participants in that weekly shopping trawl would have guessed the contents of the bag we had stashed at our booted feet.

"Actually, I think we'd all identify more as nihilists. Now fuck off."

The alarm is deafening, and the fire door has swung shut behind us, imprisoning us inside without the vital tools to escape. For long seconds, my heart pounds in time to the searing klaxon as we race around the upstairs bar like rats in a trap.

"The window! We can jump back out the window!"

We try to lever it up, jamming it against the air conditioning unit. The drop down into the alley is an ankle-smashing ten metres, but somewhere in my fear-frazzled brain this seems logical.

"Call someone from outside!"

"They can't do the climb up to the window!"

"Fuck! Fuck! Fuck!"

"Are we trapped? Who closed the door?"

"Does it fucking matter? How do we get it open?"

"Where are the tools?"

"Just keep taping the fucking sensors!"

Even through my amphetamine-addled senses, the irony of becoming locked inside a building we had wished to open, and then secure, was not lost on me. It felt almost like a trap had been set, anticipating our arrival, a snare tightening and a set of metal jaws snapping shut.

Suddenly the fire door opens, and the innocent face of Barnabas comes through it, grinning like a schoolboy who's just robbed the tuck shop.

"Why's everyone shouting so much?"

"DON'T SHUT THAT DOOR!"

Once the alarms quieten, exhausted and frustrated by their futile cries, we explore the darkness, locating fuse boxes and examining piles of debris.

By the door is a glaring void where the painting depicting Mother Black Cunt used to hang, looted by tomb-raiding property developers no doubt.

"MOTHER BLACK CUNT IS BACK – AND SHE'S PISSED OFF!"

A day later, we deal with the police, who are dimissed once satisfied we have occupied the Black Cunt legally, and that it was now a civil dispute between us and the owners.

A week of cleaning floors and locking doors, then we throw them open to the crowds to celebrate her return for one final night of debauchery.

The girl on stage is re-enacting the stations of the cross – maybe she gets the Crass reference, maybe not – but it seems like it has never been interpreted quite like this. She dances a furious pop-jazz ensemble to pounding hip-hop rhythms, stripping down to a giant pair of Y-fronts and tube socks. She squats on the face of her disciples as they prostrate across the back of one another, and then squirts water from her vagina into the faces of the braying audience. Now, she sits astride a chair, her fist inserted into her cunt, legs splayed in the air, pumping herself like some giant meat-puppet. Perhaps it's fitting. This is indeed a resurrection, and a crucifixion, but a queer, feminist one, that also ultimately ends in sacrifice, and the death of a legend.

Behind her, Pinky bounces in her sparkly glitter bra and the gigantic sound engineer whoops and cheers as I watch from the wings with the other acts, feeling glorious in my Dutch milkmaid outfit of a gingham pinafore and ginger wig, complete with cap, pigtails and gimp mask.

Journalists mill through the crowds, taking quotes from flamboyantly decked out party-goers:

> *It's not just about sexuality – it's about space. Where do the queers go, the punks, the marginalised and disenfranchised? These are the peoples that made Camden, created a zone where people could be what they wanted to be. There is no space left for us here. The bougies are squeezing us out like pus from a spot.*

"We're here, we're queer, we're anarchists, we'll fuck you up!"

The Black Cunt is an embodiment of queer history, past, present and future, packed with a melange of old regulars and new faces from the squat collective. Tattoos and bare flesh, wild eye make-up and hair extensions, clean-cut twinks and hairy bears, butch femmes and mohawked crusties – a riot of sexualities and modifications and bizarre, wondrous in-betweens and ambiguities. Male and female collapse into one another and back out the other side. The dance floor is packed, heaving with bodies grinding and bouncing against one another in a sweaty, amorphous confusion, or effortlessly whirling around like protons and electrons blasted free from the bonds of physics. Disco balls twirl in the gloom above and a row of plasma screens play porno featuring a man with penises for hands.

I came here as a 20-year-old in the eighties and there were older gay people here, queer people. That gave me a sense of history, that I belong somewhere to a culture. I learnt a lot about my queer history from places like this. It's essential that we don't lose that.

The first half of the night features a smattering of anarchist poetry that prompted a passionate intervention by a short-haired woman called Abigail who decries the appropriation of queer culture by outsiders. I throw the microphone to her to allow her to voice her upset.

"This is a queer space for queer people, and we've got this cunt on stage talking about men he admires!"

I can't deny it. My poetry had praised John Cooper Clarke, Alfredo Bonnano and, in my defence, Emma Goldman, but perhaps in such a fast-paced style that people could not catch every reference. It was simple enough to solve. Give the mike to the mikeless, a voice to the voiceless.

Abigail shares her story with us. "The last two years we've been regular and being a tranny, point is, you're so welcome. I swear to God we haven't been welcome anywhere like this have we? I swear. Nowhere. You don't have to be gay, you don't have to be lesbian. Everybody's welcome. And that's the Black Cunt, that's what it's all about."

Other acts smash laptops on stage to the tune of *"I Can't Live If Living Is Without You"*, sing Subhumans lyrics over cheesy pop backing tracks, or dress in drag and perform Class War anthems with trios of old crusties, bulging genitalia flashing through skimpy black panties and stockings.

> *Camden used to be a land of punks, poor artists, squatters, sometimes all in one. Once upon a time a squat in Camden would not cause a headline nor an eyelid battering and now that's no longer the case. The squatters should be welcomed back to Camden – they were part of what made it what it is today.*

Oberon White opens the second half. He waits in the wings, but there is something wrong. No matter how I introduce him, he refuses to enter the stage, and I am left floundering and laughing before a rolling rabble of reprobates. He is mummified, tissues and cloth wrapped around his head and arms. Maybe he is blind and cannot see me. I introduce him again, like a skipping record, and then flee the stage to let him sort it out. Lurking by the dressing room, the murmurs of an expectant crowd are deafening in my ears. Slowly, he raises his arms and staggers zombie-like on to the stage to peals of squealing violins. His assistant scampers on behind, and slowly unwinds the bandages from around him. Underneath, he is ethereal, ghostly face painted in a skull rictus, a Pierrot-clown with a black tear dripping from one kohl-rimmed eye. As he is unveiled, he begins to sing in a sweet operatic tenor, the crisp clear sonorous notes slicing through the sudden smoky silence of the bar.

> *So what is wanted in Camden? A load of rich investors in sterile flats? I'm sick of amazing buildings and venues being taken over by*

"developers". And before you ask, I run a business here and have done for 20 years, I am totally opposed to the gentrification.

As he sings, his assistant begins to unwind a clothesline hung with black and white portraits of victims of sexual violence: people persecuted for being queer in Russia, in the Ukraine, in Kenya, in Malaysia, people beaten and jailed and murdered for their sexual orientation. Pictures of the fresh-faced Jody Dobrowski – murdered on Clapham Common in 2005 by thugs who suspected him to be gay; an image of the Admiral Duncan pub in Soho, bombed in May 1999, by a former British National Party member, killing three people and wounding at least 70; of Giovanna Del Nord, a 46-year-old trans woman, attacked minutes after entering The Market Tavern in Leicester, without warning punched in the head and knocked unconscious; of Steven Simpson, an autistic, openly gay 18-year-old, who had homophobic slurs written on his body and was set on fire at his birthday party. All the while, the only sound remaining is the sonorous tenor of the crying clown and the wailing lament of violins behind him.

I'm a Camden resident and a few weeks ago while walking home, I witnessed something going on in the doorway of the Black Cunt between a man and woman where the woman was screaming being pushed up against the door in the doorway. Others were intervening and I didn't want to get into a threatening situation, but I waved down a passing police car and asked them to go and investigate.

All through the wild melee of the night, the police kept coming round, checking in on us, but with the in-house sound system having built-in limiters and a closed-door policy, they had more than enough drama dealing with the herds of thrill-seekers ploughing the trail up and down between Chalk Farm and Mornington Crescent. The queer scene has had a culture of resistance since the days of Stonewall and the Gay Liberation Front – we felt confident that tonight we had reclaimed for ourselves a space in the heart of Camden.

> *The area around the Black Cunt is quiet and a perfect spot for far more serious and damaging crimes than squatters would commit. I urge Camden police to allow Camden Queer Punx 4Eva to stay in the Black Cunt until they can agree what will be done going forward. As a member of the Queer community and a Camden local – I wish the Queer Punx well.*

One old-timer told us some history:

> *When the Black Cunt used to be split in two, there was a faux-wall between the front and back to hide the sodomites from the prying eyes of Babylon. Symbolically, the wall came down as the law and the culture changed. It is easy to forget that within living memory homosexuality was a crime. Times have liberalised, but also become less radical. Still this space – our space – is under attack from the creeping tentacles of gentrification.*

A queer-punk painted up to look like a cat chipped in: "The Black Cunt used to be so fucking mainstream. I never used to go there. Just middle-class, bougie as fuck. Mug gay yuppies!"

We lose in court, of course, the judge upholding the claimant's case that we were trespassers, and granting them possession of the building forthwith. At eight o'clock the next morning, High Court enforcers crowbar the door and inform us that we have been evicted. A man in a zebra-print miniskirt with hoop earrings and an Alsatian on a string stands reading to the newly homeless crowd from a long scroll.

"And so, Mother Black Cunt joins the ranks of the fallen across London, as yet more LGBT venues succumb to the curse of gentrification. RIP, dear Mother, in this incarnation born 1965, died 2015."

A skinhead female next to him, two white rats climbing about her breasts, is furious, berating his every utterance.

"Queer liberation, not queer consumerism!"

Out in the street, Camden is stirring, shoppers and commuters streaming towards the tube station across the road. As we sit on our collection of luggage, sleeping bags and feather boas, I look south towards the city. Sliding along the road towards us is a lumpen old lady, wrapped in diaphanous veils and cardigans of heavy-knit wool, pushing a trolley laden with treasures wrapped in plastic.

"She joins Madame Jojo, formerly of Soho, who opened her doors and her legs to many a punter and many a good time, from 1966 to 2014."

Atop the crone's rolling pile, a mangy cat sits regally cleaning its genitals, a slender leg arched towards the clear blue skies. She approaches, the repetitive creak of one wheel growing louder and louder as she drags herself and her possessions towards us. Her face looks like rotting fruit left too long in the sun, the skin slack and riddled with spidery red veins, in shocking contrast to the thick electric blue arteries that stand like electrical cable between the delicate avian bones of her hands. She shuffles, seemingly held erect by her trolley, as if engaging in a slow-motion collapse all the way down the length of the Camden High Street.

"The fire will not consume us! We take it and make it our own!"

"And let us not forget those stubborn bastions of mutual cock-sucking, clit-tickling, sodomy and feverish buggery: the Coleherne, 1955 to 2010, and the King Edward VI of Brompton, 1966 to 2011."

She pulls up alongside us, her breath wheezing, and turns a pair of eyes like pebbles in a dish of red rice towards us, peering out at us from the folded skin of her face. Her trolley stands a scant inch from the shoe of a Metropolitan police officer who has attended to ensure there is no breach of the peace. Her scarf, purple and black, is a fleshy wattle hanging from under her chin. She waits, timeless, patient as the ages, turning her gaze towards the uniformed man before her.

"Out of the way, copper!"

The officer leaps around, startled, and backs out of the way, nearly falling into the road in his surprise. A wry smile twists the blue lips, and she angles a gleeful glance towards us.

"Mugs, all of you."

She departs, slipping between bailiffs and commuters and off towards Chalk Farm. She looks like she has been here since 1751 – a vision of Mother Black Cunt herself, timeless, eternally wandering these streets, the Crone of Camden, as defiant and unstoppable as ever, rejected and reviled, yet as integral to these streets as the stones themselves. As she goes I turn my gaze skyward, looking up at the facade of the Black Cunt.

"The Little Apple, Nelson's Head, Man Bar, Candy, Blush, the G-A-Y, all struck down in the flush of their youth and growing maturity. Whither next for the fags and the dykes? Where shall all the homos go? And what fate awaits the trannies and the benders? They are sexually cleansing the boroughs of London – first Soho, now Camden. Are we all to be forced to accept the high street's tepid and limp offerings – like kittens licking skimmed milk from capitalism's turgid dugs? Are we forced to become vanilla – acceptable, so long as we cause no trouble – our sexuality and our lifestyle choices just another option within consumerism? We are here, we are queer, where can we have a beer?"

The rainbow flag is being dragged inside by a lumpen bailiff hanging out the window. The effigy of a banker in a suit slumps limply beside it. He is unceremoniously pulled within. The hand-painted cardboard sign falls from his limp plastic hands, and the words "I $OLD CAMDEN" slap down on to a pavement at the booted feet of a High Court Enforcer. I sigh, and begin to gather up my possessions, wondering where there might be space for me now.

"WE DON'T WANT EQUAL RIGHTS – WE WANT REVENGE!"

11

The Shittest Picnic Ever

The poetry of the earth is never dead.
John Keats

Eyelids stuttering like a caught-out politician's, I take long moments to breathe on the mattress in the guest room. The sun is blazing through the high windows, hitting the bitter graffiti we scrawled on the mezzanine in drunken rebelliousness: *"Whilst you plenum, we crack buildings"*. Mierda is already gone, no doubt down in the yard putting the finishing touches to the mural. Grizzly sits in the corner of the room, looking at me patiently, awaiting my next move.

It has been two weeks here in Rigaerstrasse, feeling the creeping comforts and stasis of the place sapping our vigour. Today is the day we leave for Hambach Forst. Battling to my shonky feet, I stumble over the bit of cord holding the sole to my shoe as I gather our booty from Italy, the zines and patches from the street-markets of Berlin, the empty bottles for recycling, retie the length of rope around the flapping sole of my boot, and check the scrawled notes on how to escape the fuck out of Berlin.

We were sat at the Rasthof Michendorf, halfway through the wine, on the brink of giving up for the night and setting up the tent, when we got picked up.

"Look, that one has Magdeburg plates. That's halfway there. Ask them."

Mierda takes a swig of red and skips over to await the two tan-skinned males as they emerge from the service station.

"Hello, excuse me, are you going to Magdeburg?"

"*Ja.*"

"Can we come with you?"

"There are two of you?"

I sit sheepishly, trying to mask the large rucksacks and Grizzly, who I am telepathically willing not to start barking at them.

"Yes."

"And you have a dog?"

"Yes."

Ah, shit. These guys are dark-skinned, black-haired, their accents suggesting an origin in the Muslim sphere. Dogs are *haram*. Their car is super shiny and sleek, some brand a gearhead would probably drool over. I begin to think about where to set the tent up.

The first guy catches the second as he emerges, and they make an exchange in rapid-fire babel. I read the body language as best I can, trying to keep my mind open.

"OK. But the dog has to go in the luggage. That ok?"

"Fine! Great!" Me and Mierda chime together, grabbing the bags and hiding the wine before they can change their minds. We sling the bags in the back, and Grizzly obediently, mysteriously silently, jumps up behind them and immediately settles down, tongue lolling happily. It's almost as if she knew. Or maybe she was as glad as we were to leave Berlin.

We leap in the back, dropping into plush leather upholstery. It smells like a rental car – new, synthetic, false. In front is a galaxy of gnomic buttons and devices, a screen showing GPS coordinates, everything illuminated in space-age neon blue. The passenger in the front has his seat almost horizontal, so me and Mierda squeeze into one half of the back seat next to each other.

The driver guns the engine, and we flee the service station like a gazelle bolting from a predator, tearing out into the *autobahn* night. The leather-upholstered seats heat up at the click of a button. Euro-techno blasts from the surround sound speakers. As the acceleration increases and the G-force kicks in, we both scramble surreptitiously for our seatbelts as we realise this driver intends to max out the capabilities of his souped-up car on the limitless potential of the autobahn.

As he drives, he smokes sickly smelling skunk in a pipe and talks over his shoulder at us. All the while, the needle creeps upwards.

100 kph.

"So you always travel like this? You have job? You have home? I live Berlin, but my family all live in the West. In Cologne."

110 kph.

"Really? You are going to Cologne? That's actually where we are going."

"Oh really?"

He talks to his passenger in rapid-fire language that we can't understand. We exchange hopeful glances.

"OK. So we take to you Cologne. No problem. This is my brother. We from Afghanistan. We come after war start there. Very bad. Very bad. Much trouble. Much violence."

120 kph.

"I make money delivering cars. Make little money. Make little survive. You come Germany, I sure you see very nice life. People nice. Life nice. Everything easy. Very good. For me, very hard. For my brother, very hard. For my family, very hard. Can be very difficult."

135 kph.

"In Afghanistan, you buy 1 kilo of heroin, 5000 Euros. Bring back to Europe. Sell 100,000 easily. Make good money. Make good life. Never work again."

150 kph.

"You want to smoke?"

170 kph.

"You believe in Allah? *SCHIESSE*!"

Actually he shouts something else, but I didn't catch it. It sounded like *sheize*. The car swerves violently, sliding dramatically to the right. As quick as a flash, he restabilises it and pulls it back to the left.

"Did you see that? Did you see? *Es war ein Hirsch, mit großen Geweihe, die wir fast traf es...*What you say in English? With... with? With these."

He actually takes both hands off the wheel and holds them to his head to demonstrate antlers. At this point his brother intervenes, saying something in sleepy but firm syllables.

"OK, he say I stop talking and concentrate on driving now."

We race on through the night in silence, me and Mierda secretly sipping the wine, then drifting off to sleep as the seats warm our thighs and the lights of the autobahn hypnotically flash by at 100 mph. We crack the window to smoke and the jet stream screams through the cabin as if we were on an airplane. As my eyelids droop I idly wonder whether Grizzly is asleep in the back on the top of several kilos of heroin from Afghanistan.

They drop us off, unceremoniously, outside a tram stop before dawn, awkwardly watching as we drag our bags and dog out the back. They notice that the boot is covered in dog hair. We look appropriately apologetic, then they are off, racing away to their families or their drug deal or to try and run over more deer. We jump the tram, looking out the window until we spot a bottle shop with a nearby park.

Sipping cold beer, we wander through a park of gelded trees, filled with dozens upon dozens of rabbits that hop, skip and nibble the pruned grass, calm and peaceful and undisturbed by our presence. Grizzly pulls on the lead, straining at them with interest, and the sky begins to turn blue above us. Bottle collectors lurk in the bushes, giving their location away by the clink of glass.

As it gets light, we pass out on the sleeping bags, dozing a few hours. We are surprised when we awake to find the rabbits and bottlers have all transformed into youth. Cologne is a major university town, and on a summer's day such as this these fresh-faced and clean-looking young folks descend upon the parks to barbecue, throw frisbees and leave behind empty beer bottles for the refugees to pick up.

They grow rowdier as it gets sunny, and not wanting to sleep another day there, we troop back down to the tram stop and jump the rest of the way to the *Hauptbanhof*. Nearly there, we spot a gang of inspectors at one of the stops and leap off to safety. Meandering through the streets, we are soon beneath the spires of the Dom.

We are waiting on the platform for the train when we are approached by a young woman dressed in black, wearing a patch of a pair of cogs with a spanner dropping between them.

"You go to the occupation?"

We smile and nod. We have found our guide.

We jump the train together, watching each other's backs, chatting all the way to the woods.

"Several of the villages around here are ghost towns now. Just shells, left up for show, awaiting the bulldozers. Old buildings, beautiful, being torn down by diggers. Same with the solar panels everywhere, the wind farms, the hundreds of thousands of Euros poured into recycling schemes and schools talks. All of it propaganda."

"Green-washing, we call it."

"It's a total cover-up. RWE just want to present a clean face to the world whilst raping it. You have to go see the Hole. It's unbelievable. I cannot even describe it. It's like Mordor."

She appears physically pained as she talks, losing herself for a moment looking out the window.

"I just went to the police station to see about our comrade who was arrested today. Ah, don't worry. The people at the camp will tell you all about it."

We pass her the wine, and we drink, sharing logistics of our various living arrangements.

"And who is this? I don't like to say pet."

"Grizzly. Our companion."

She ruffles Grizzly's fur affectionately. Grizzly seems pleased, parking herself beneath the seats of the train.

"Do you ever have any trouble jumping the train?"

"Not if there is three or four of us. They normally don't think it's worth the problem."

It is a long walk through the pitch-blackness of the countryside – I doubt we could've found it without Grasshalm. When we arrive, a dreadlocked man named Graeme gives us a breathless update.

"Ah so you're here for the festival? Good, good. Well, we're all a bit tired today, as we had an eviction. The tower. Remy's Tower, it's called, was raided by the police. One guy got arrested; he's at the station now. He threw a bucket of shit at the cops. One of them twisted his neck apparently so it's assault. All a bit of a palaver. It was the last living barricade and all. Fourteen hours it took them. They took him because he had 'no social obligations' in Germany, and was 'likely to stay away from trial'. We have to rebuild the barricades tomorrow, but the tower has gone. Such a shame. So you're staying a bit are you? Well, you're welcome to camp in the forest, be aware that it's illegal, or you can put your stuff down in the meadow if you like."

As I sit and shit in the little compost toilet hut, a hazel dormouse peeks out from a pallet dumped next to the sawdust bag. Its cute little eyes peer at me with curious innocence. I look out into the forest, the sounds of birds singing and the branches of tall, elegant trees rustling, and I realise that I know the names of almost nothing. The forest is comprised of pines, yew, oak. I have spotted dockleafs and clover, nettles and brambles, but to the vast majority of its diversity I am ignorant. I guess most people are nowadays, the herblore and arboreal knowledge that would have been natural for our ancestors is now forgotten. The contents of the vast fields around the encampment are more easily recognisable: endless monocultural rows of potato, cauliflower, waving stands of maize, uniform, relentless, armies of doubtless genetically mutated aliens. Whole fields of hybrid triffids, ready to take over the world once everyone has gone blind from staring at some mysterious meteor.

Fifteen and more centuries ago, Germany was covered in mixed forest like this, home to a weald society of hunters, foragers, gatherers and natural farmers. The forest abounded with deer, squirrel, pigeon, fowl, not to mention a host of challengers to the dominance of man – wolves, bears, boar – real life monsters of the time. Perhaps that's where so much of the modern-day hatred of nature comes from – that for so long it was seen as a killer and enemy. The natives would have been expert herbalists, naming and knowing hundreds and more of plants for their medicinal and healing qualities. Now this weird vagabond camp sits on a meadow on the edge of the last patch of a 12,000-year-old forest, and the lack of connection is apparent. In four years it will all be gone – the hazel dormouse and the history, the centuries-old yew and oak, the brief moments of liberty on the fringe of oblivion.

Dumping a handful of sawdust down the hole, I pull up my shorts and tuck my leggings into the top of my socks. This is tick country, which means Lyme disease. We had already pulled a number of the purple-grey sacs out of Grizzly's knotted fur and were keen to avoid becoming a meal ourselves.

I stroll back through the forest, manoeuvring around the barricades of branches and logs that have been constructed across the pathways. One has been decorated with a large red "A", and a road sign woven into its mesh has been spray-painted with slogans, "ELF" and "*Hambach Bleibt!*" The soil of the truck-paths is solid, compacted, grossly different in consistency to the spongey, yielding layers of leaf litter and humus of the forest proper. It even smells different – wafts of organic, living matter erupting from each step, like the breath of the trees. I walk back through Oaktown, gazing up at the precipitously positioned treehouses, 20 metres above in the boughs of the trees. A man in a harness is setting up the ropes to clamber above and spend the day in peaceful meditation with his tree. He waves cheerfully to me as I pass, hopping over a trio of tractor tyres laden with rubble. I jump again as soon as I land, narrowly avoiding crushing a miniature dance-hall of dung beetles rolling their treasures around.

The forest ends abruptly at the meadow occupation, marked by a man in an elf hat sat in a tree playing a mandolin and singing softly: "*I want to be/forever punk/I want to be/forever punk...*" I pass through the freegan kitchen, into the low hut of the kitchen proper. A few people talk softly in German, preparing tofu and *brotchen* from the packed metal containers. They have a full wheelie bin of soya-products, donated by supporters and shipped from Cologne. In the meadow, a small fire burns by the dining tables, and beyond, the narrow strip between two fields of wheat is littered with caravans, roundhouses of timber and, towards the airstrip, a number of straw-bale houses and hobbit-huts, partially sunk into the ground.

It looks like a crew of nomadic space-pirates were marooned here on the shore and spent their time trying to organise without their captain. The dozen or so constructions are idiosyncratic, an eco-refugee camp of wattle walls, pallet structures, insulation; a hybrid of plastic functionality and ecological innovation. Red and black antifascist flags fly from makeshift poles alongside ragged rainbow strings of Tibetan prayer flags. Hand-painted tarps are everywhere: "*Ohne Mampf, keinen Kampf*" by the kitchen, "Refugees Welcome" by the tool shed. The walls of the kitchen bear various signs of instruction to wash hands, close lids because of rats, no meat, no smoking, and in between, the scraps of calendars and rotas and propaganda blur to become an anti-authoritarian collage. Dreamcatchers spin in the breeze next to mobiles of pinecones and wool. Wicker baskets and water jugs are piled by the tool shed, next to a plastic dog with its face smashed off and boxes and boxes of weirdly wonderful, perhaps one day useful, *stuff*.

Behind fences of wood lashed together with rope, people are growing miniature gardens of herbs, sage, lemon balm, mint and parsley. I run my hands over the delicate leaves, feeling the differences, smelling deeply of each one as I pass. Beside one hobbit house, its roof layered with clods of turf and straw, tall stacks of sunflower are in regal bloom, their innards already filling with seed. In another, shared between the solar-powered "technology caravan" and someone's private van, a cacophony of broccoli is beginning to delicately emerge, beans hang bountiful stacks of pods from their runners, pumpkins are swelling, nasturtiums flirt with the bees with their spicy flowers of vermilion, orange and yellow. The gardens are marked out with old jam jars and glass bottles, rows of gleaming white, green and brown surrounding the lush stands of intermingled plants. A row of solar panels gleams futuristically, surrounded by terracotta pots of cacti and salads. The infoshop is decorated with old vinyl records, a gasmask with a pair of antlers sprouting from it, the simple slogan *"COAL KILLS"* next to a stuffed pheasant staring arrogantly back at me from the walls. A small boy with cornflower blue eyes and hair so blond it looks white in the sunlight plays with a plastic truck in the sandpit. I watch him for a while as he moves dirt around, wondering if the men driving the big diggers over on the other side of the highway had once been the same. Just kids playing in the sand.

Brightly coloured murals and slogans mark the passage of a multitude of defiant artists. Mierda has been working on the outside of the library/freeshop structure – the outlines emerge of a naked woman swinging down from a tree to smash the face of a man wielding a chainsaw. Strolling further along, I spot her atop the tower at the entrance to the meadow. She is unwinding a huge red and black flag from its pole, the wind catching it and flicking it out against the blue sky. I realise with a smile that it is a German flag with the gold torn from the bottom – a symbolic removal of wealth, to leave behind the black of anarchy and the blood of the people. She turns and waves cheerily to me from her viewpoint as a crop-duster soars into the sky from the airstrip behind her.

We gather in the open-sided forum hut. The sun is setting over the fields of monoculture outside. Grizzly slips in and lies down expectantly, the little pup Hanuc bothering her experimentally. We laugh that we have a friend of the same name back in London. The projector screen lights up the faces of a dozen or so smiling, patient people who chat and smoke whilst awaiting the speaker to begin.

"Thank you all for coming. I will try to talk about the occupation here, first giving some background on the situation then detailing some of the various actions and resistance over the last three years.

"The remaining Hambach forest – originally part of a 6000-hectare old-growth forest – is ecologically unique in Europe. For more than 30 years the energy corporation RWE has been cutting it down. Today, less than 500 hectares remain. All of it is to be cut down to make space for the mine in the years to come – at least these are the plans of RWE and the government.

"All this because underneath the forest one finds the so called 'brown gold'. Lignite has been exploited in the Rhineland between Aachen and Cologne for more than a hundred years. In 1970 a large-scale lignite extraction project was approved. This project included three huge open cast pits, the extension of existing as well as the construction of new coal power plants, and the development of the necessary infrastructure.

"We have been in occupation of the forest since April 2012,

when the last action of a *klimacamp* held in the area was to occupy the forest. The *klimacamps* in the Rhineland were inspired by the UK's climate camps, which seem to be much more developed than here in Germany. Or at least they used to be, I don't know how they are now. Of the four major coal mine areas in Deutschland, the one here is the largest, covering 80 square kilometres and being half a kilometre deep at its lowest point. RWE have been pumping out water for years, lowering the water table and endangering the forest. They have been buying up land and villages for decades, building on a project that was started by Hitler and the Nazis before the war, discontinued for several decades afterwards, and then resumed in the 70s by RWE. They have been buying the houses of all the villages in the area, on the condition that those who sell do not discuss how much they are paid with each other. This allows RWE to negotiate individually rather than collectively, separating the villagers and ensuring a stronger position for them. They are building new villages in the area to rehouse people, but they all look like they are from Super Mario. Many historic beautiful buildings are being destroyed, and the locals being bought off with schools-for-land programmes.

"RWE spends a huge amount of money on security to protect their mining operation, as well as investing hundreds of thousands in surveillance of the occupation and propaganda in the villages to turn the locals against us. You've probably seen all the solar panels and wind farms, as well as the new *autobahn* to route traffic past Buir without allowing anyone to see what they are doing. RWE also subsidise a lot of the farmers around here, creating an image of abundance and ideal countryside life, whilst behind the screen of trees they are destroying this area.

"2012 was their first eviction attempt. We had dug a tunnel, six metres deep, which I have a model of here. You can see there are three levels, with a fire door locked on the first level. They had to chop through this with an axe. Then there is a descent to a smaller tunnel, and then another level, to an even smaller tunnel and a store-room where we stayed. There was food and water here, and a few buckets for piss and shit.

"This tunnel held out for three days, during which time jeeps and vans owned by the police and security drove over the top. You could feel the ground shaking. It didn't feel very safe. All the time above people were blasting the Tetris theme tune through speakers. The tunnel held out for three days.

"Six hundred police turned up for the eviction. The photos don't really do it justice. After we were evicted from there, a local farmer allowed us to move into the meadow occupation, and we have been here since then, despite the security and the police harassing us, arresting him and threatening him, he still allows us to stay here as it is his land. RWE work very hard to convince the villagers that we are evil, that we are drug addicts and thieves and whatever. But many of them are now realising what they have lost by believing RWE. Many support us more and more for the occupation. Now they are trying to evict us and demolish the buildings here as we do not have zoning permission. It is relentless.

"Hambachforst and the Burgewald – the 'guaranteed forests' – doesn't really exist anymore. They certainly aren't guaranteed. They used to cover this entire area on the map, and consisted of mixed forest of pines, beech, oaks. Trees that don't normally grow together have found harmony here over 12,000 years. The forest is home to a number of endangered species, including the hazel dormouse, which you may have seen running around in the kitchens, the middle-spotted woodpecker and Bechstein's bat. Also at night we can walk through the forest and see a number of fluorescent mushrooms. It's really quite beautiful.

"So this is a picture of the Monkeytown occupation. There were four treehouses, at a height of 18 to 25 metres from the ground. The treehouses are really quite cosy, quite safe, and people would live in them almost constantly, waiting for something to happen. Here you can see a big net connecting a number of trees, the idea being that if they cut one tree or one rope, then the people in the net will be harmed. There is not a lot to do, mainly waiting, a lot of time with nothing happening, and then suddenly the eviction comes. The tree you live in becomes your friend, you spend time with it every day. It lasted for seven months, in which time there were 30 barricade removals, kitchen removals. Of course eviction day is rebuilding day. But even using the dead wood from the forest is a problem, as the forest relies on the dead wood to be healthy.

"After seven months, the security and police arrived to evict Monkeytown. The people in the trees locked on, climbed into the nets, used rope links. The eviction took from 8am till 10pm. The police came with cherry-pickers for those in the trees. All you can hear from up there is screaming, the sound of machinery, chainsaws. You can't see anything. All of Monkeytown was clear-cut that winter. Here's a photo of a 400-year-old beech being cut down. Here's another one of a 200-year oak.

"So we still organise direct actions against the Hole, encouraging people to do what they feel comfortable with. Here's a photo of people sabotaging one of the diggers. Here's an orchestra that came, playing in front of one of the diggers. Here's people chaining themselves to the railway. This was one of the first actions, and even though it only lasted a few hours, as they cut through the locks very quickly, it still delayed the shipments of coal and cost RWE thousands of Euros. Here are some of us up on the tower of the digger.

"So even with all this, it is estimated that the total clearance of Hambachforst will be complete within four years.

"Maybe I can show you some videos before the battery runs out, and then you can ask questions if anybody has any. Here you can see one of the raids by security. One guy actually threatens to kill us if we damage his machines. You wouldn't believe it if we didn't have footage of it. These people. I don't understand them. They laugh and make jokes whilst the trees come down. They don't seem human sometimes."

He grows visibly emotional as he talks, lapsing into a moment of silence. The pressure must be unbearable. I feel like a tourist.

Someone asks a question, but the only one I have in my mind is, "What hope do you have?"

But it is an impossible question to ask. He has to have hope, all these people here have to have hope of some kind, but it seems utterly hopeless. What they are up against is so huge and relentless and faceless and unstoppable, and somehow so many people support it, buy into it, surrender their humanity in order to see it continue. They sign it off as their job, the only option, and those who are against it as some kind of crazy crusties and miscreants. Yet surely anyone could see how invaluable this place is, and how lignite is just fucking evil. This was the frontline of the war against ecocide, against the madness of capitalist logic, for the salvation of the planet, and it did not look like they were winning.

"How do you know if someone's a vegan? They'll fucking tell you."

"Did you ever hear of a guy called Barry Horne?

"He was from Northampton – where I'm from – though I never met him of course. Went to an ALF meeting at 35 years old and pow – that was it. Became vegetarian, started sabbing hunts around Cambridge. Went to Florida to free a dolphin that was held in captivity in a tiny pond, on its own. Dolphins are extremely social animals. A cell of them spent nights sneaking in, getting to know it, before finally jumping in with a giant dolphin stretcher. Only realised then that there was no way they could lift a 650-pound dolphin out of the park. They got nicked on the way back to the car by local coppers…Couldn't explain why they had that stretcher.

"Still, they kept campaigning, leafleting, protesting, raising money. Eventually raised 120,000 pounds and bought him off the zoo. Released him after some rehabilitation, and within days he'd joined a pod. Imagine that – taking a dolphin from captivity all the way through to seeing it leaping through the water with all its mates.

"He didn't stop there. He ended up in prison, possession of explosives. Sentenced to three years. He only got more hardcore inside. Listen to this:

> *The animals continue to die and the torture goes on in greater and greater measure. People's answer to this? More vegeburgers, more Special Brew and more apathy. There is no longer any Animal Liberation Movement. That died long ago. All that is left is a very few activists who care, who understand and who act...If you don't act then you condone. If you don't fight then you don't win. And if you don't win then you are responsible for the death and suffering that will go on and on.*

"Soon as he got out, he went on the warpath. Firebombs, all over the country, a one-man cell targeting the cosmetics industry, Boots, the high-street face of GlaxoSmithKline, in Bristol, the Isle of Wight, all over. He got caught. He knew he would, but for him it was a war. Eighteen years. Eighteen fucking years for arson against property, nobody injured. They called him a terrorist. He used to be a bin-man. Whilst inside he did four hunger strikes – 35 days, 46 days, 68 days – no food. Whilst on-strike, the Animal Rights Militia – the ones who did not support nonviolence – went out to war in his name. They dug tunnels outside Huntingdon Life Sciences to prevent eviction; they raided guinea pig farms, rabbit farms, mink farms; they blockaded Dover and drove a car into Parliament Square, slashing its tyres and d-locking to the steering wheel. Four hundred people marched on a primate holding facility near Brighton. It was a fucking insurrection.

"Here's another good one:

the fight is not for us, not for our personal wants and needs. It is for every animal that has ever suffered and died in the vivisection labs, and for every animal that will suffer and die in those same labs unless we end this evil business now. The souls of the tortured dead cry out for justice, the cry of the living is for freedom. We can create that justice and we can deliver that freedom. The animals have no one but us. We will not fail them.

"He died fighting. His last hunger strike lasted 15 days, before his liver shut down. The media vilified him. Sipping sweet tea to survive was turned into 'a feast'. They mocked him because he terrified them, because he was relentless, because he was ethically above them all. He was a fucking hero.

"So eat your meat and laugh at the vegans. And go fuck yourself whilst you're at it."

Through the remnant of forest, past the ramshackle barricades, already being rebuilt by a lone woodsman, likely to be stripped within a day, and over the road. Clambering over the pile of sand dumped to block the access to the abandoned highway. We linger there on the dual carriageway, looking at the weeds peeking through the asphalt, staring at the dead signs, forever blank above the empty roadways. Abandoned by civilisation, it is for a moment as if humanity had disappeared from the face of the planet, and Mierda and I and Grizzly and a few darting starlings all that remain behind. As we head further into the west, the signs of the civilised return. We dodge a roving security car by ducking down behind a copse of reeds and tall grass that has erupted between the metal barriers. We follow a dump-truck as it cruises over a bridge above the highway. Soon, the ground around us becomes stripped of trees, then of bushes, and finally only grasses and tangled brush struggle to survive amidst acres of crushed and flattened dirt. Our boots slip and slide through sand. Not even soil. Just dead, compacted dirt, with clumps of dying grass, stunted seedlings and scrawny thistles meekly squirming between the hillocks. Even here, nature battles on, but on the horizon, behind piles of disrupted and destroyed earth, the ground suddenly drops away, revealing the cavernous scar of the Hole, and no sign of growth remains.

Its scale is hard to put into words. It is Dune – desert planet – you could expect to see giant worms bursting from the ground and hordes of Fremen charging across it. A train line runs in perfect parallel to the cliff drop we stand on, slicing across the barren soil unbroken. Not 100 metres away from us is the monstrous bagger machine. Its size is gargantuan, alien, a mechanical monster hundreds of feet high, the great rotating disk like ten JCBs strapped into a circle, relentlessly scooping the cliffside, pulling away tons of sand and subsoil 24 hours a day, groaning and murmuring like a slaving demon in the depths of hell. Lights gleam on its scaffold tower, and the tiny figure operating it looks like an ant on the side of some vast steel scarecrow. It looks like the gateway to Hades, like the surface of the moon, like a bomb went off and evaporated all forms of life for 80 square kilometres around it.

Across a barren plain of dead soil, between us and the distant hills, is a void, a lacuna of absent earth like a meteor crater blasted into the ground. One day, once the lignite is stripped from the earth, they will fill the crater with water and sail boats on top of it – the final insult of turning a rape victim into a playground for the rich. In the distance, the funnels of power plants choke the dusk sky with plumes of smoke. Above us, the moon burns as a flaming diamond amidst clouds streaked in violet, aquamarine, cerise and vermilion. I wonder how much of the spectacle of colours of the iridescent sunset is caused by the pollutants they are releasing. On the far side, wind towers jut from the tops of hills, a paltry token of green energy next to the ravages around us.

"One day this will swallow the rest of the forest, right up to where the meadow occupation is."

"It looks like one day it will swallow the whole world."

In silence, we turn around and head back to the forest to drink ourselves into oblivion around the campfire. In the darkness, we fuck against a tree, and for a moment it feels like I am having sex with nature herself, one last desperate union before we are forced apart again.

"Even here, look at it. All this used to be trees and forest, and even in the two years since it was clear-cut, look at nature trying to fight back, trying to reclaim it, to struggle on. Look at the soil. That's 12,000 years of leaves and wood and rot and life. That's humus, baby, that is the good shit. With that, eventually a whole forest will regrow here, given enough time. The problem is now its naked, exposed. It'll bake in the heat, blow away with the wind, wash-off with water, but if they leave the plants long enough they'll recolonise it and bring it back to life."

"The clouds," Naiad said. "I thought it was pollution. The brown in the air."

"It's dust. Soil. Earth. But look at what they are doing to it. They won't leave it alone, they are ripping the soil off the planet. Literally annihilating the top-soil and replacing it with that. Sand. Dead mineral. No organic matter. No seeds. No life. Just total oblivion. Nothing will ever grow on it again. It will be totally dead."

"By 2050, there will be more plastic by weight in the oceans than fish," said Mierda. "I don't even want to be alive to see it."

"It feels like we are creating an environment that wants to kill us in self-defence."

I want to run back to the forest, to safety. Here, the sun burns our skin, the dust chokes us and the threat of discovery is constant. We sit on the stump of a 70-year-old tree, counting the rings and trying to appreciate 70 years of life and its brutal end.

Grizzly digs in the humus, a biologist, an adventurer, a

delightful curiosity, scooping deeper and deeper with her fat front paws, sticking her smiling face deeper and deeper into the thick, black soil that she removes from under the layer of leaf litter that still remains, paper-thin, covering the rich heritage of rot and growth beneath. Her snout, ears, head and finally she is able to disappear up to her shoulders and still the soil comes out, reeking of fertility and potential.

On the other side, the giant bagger machines whirl and groan, tearing vast chunks from the sides of the Hole. The forest seems like little more than a shore these days, caught between the ever-advancing hole on one side and the endless monoculture of the others.

No wonder everyone in the camp looked so burnt out, so hollow-eyed, so crushed. We'd lived in London under threat of eviction for months at a time, in a building we always knew we would never get to keep, but here they were fighting for living things, for nurturing beings and sentient creatures, and yet yearly they were losing, metre by metre, the forest disappearing into emptiness.

And then Grizzly is choking, Grizzly is foaming at the mouth and retching and yakking, clawing at her snout and gasping, drool roping through her muddy maw to drip into the hole she has been scratching. It's as if the very earth has poisoned her. Now Mierda's panicking, and Naiad, and we're all stood grabbing at Grizzly who coughs and splutters and resists. Naiad sits on her. I pull open her jaws. Mierda is trying to see if there is something stuck in her throat. They are crying, panicking, voices becoming high and keening and we can see Grizzly dying right in front of us, see Grizzly getting murdered in this forest graveyard, see us burying her in the very hole she has dug, digging her own grave.

Grizzly's jaws snap shut on my fingers and I scream, seeing blood leak from the tips, and I yell at Mierda to hold her fucking jaws open and then I am shoving my whole hand down into Grizzly's throat, trying to find the rock or the stick or whatever it is that is blocking it, but there is nothing.

"I can't find anything. I can't find it."

"Just wait. Stay calm. Look."

What a nightmare, Grizzly is going to die here in this raped forest and all we can do is watch and panic. This fucking place. How much longer before she dies? How much longer do we have to watch?

Then, we see it. Stuck to the roof of her mouth. A fat wedge of mud and soil.

We scoop it out, and Grizzly lies panting at our feet, breathing raggedly, tongue lolling like a hunk of bacon out of her mouth.

"See. She's fine. It's all fine."

"This is the shittest picnic ever."

We stroke her and wait. Within minutes she is back up and smiling at us with incoherent delight, not a care in the world, frolicking between the ragged tree-stumps and sniffing at the soil.

We pack up the picnic, and relentlessly begin to head towards the Hole, driven by some morbid desire to look into the depths of its lacuna and find some meaning to the madness. We cross the huge false dunes of compacted earth, battling through scraggly brush and grasses, Naiad and Mierda flopping ineffectively along in their flip-flops.

"This is why we came here."

We are slow, clumsy, exhausted yet still driven on, the forest receding behind us, unnervingly further and further, and we as small and lonely apes crossing the desert into oblivion.

At last, we reach the edge and the brim of the vast crater carved into the earth. In the distance, the bagger churns relentlessly, and the moonscape stretches before us, crossed by great silver railway lines. The slopes on the far side are stripped barren and bare.

In that moment, I want to see the bagger machine burn. I

want to see Molotovs fly and hit its sides, I want to fill the air with even more toxic billowing clouds of oily filth, and hear the metal scream as it collapses. I want to attack it with crowbar and bolt croppers, shred the copper from its wires and strip the steel with tooth and claw. I want to see flocks of birds slam against the glass and shred the worker mindlessly raping the planet. I want to watch a galaxy of explosions ripple across its innards and collapse its metal skeleton into the sand to turn orange with rust so that in years to come children can come play amongst the crumbling wreckage and look misty eyed at their parents as they explain: "It was here that we finally said enough."

"George! Get down!"

A little yellow digger truck is crossing the desert, a micro-machine far below us, and for some reason, I cannot move. I stand, frozen and overwhelmed, suddenly losing all reason and waving like some oogly tourist at the distant truck. It even beeps its horn at us.

"Oh shit."

I realise we have fucked up.

We stop, Mierda tired from limping up and down, and slump in the dirt to argue and bicker pettily about nothing. When we start again, the security trucks are already there up ahead between us and the safety of the forest. We are still barrelling straight towards them.

"Just keep going."

I guess my logic is that of when the security guards at a Tesco's attempt to stop you with strong words and you have to challenge them to escalate to physical interaction. Of course, the security guards at Tesco's haven't spent four years with an outlaw anarchist camp outside their front door and yearly invasions of thousands of people surging in dressed in white overalls to try to shut down the bakery department.

The nearest guard grabs me by the collar, but I won't stop and soon we are whirling in a clumsy waltz as I refuse to stop moving, attempting to twist around to break free. I see Mierda and Naiad stopping as the guards, about seven of them, close around us in their matching hi-viz armour.

"Get off me! We just went for a shit picnic!"

"We're lost!"

I start repeating our cover story, but I don't like how the three guards close nearer around me.

"George, stop!" cries Mierda. I can hear Grizzly barking.

"No, keep going!"

"Stop where you are! What are you doing here?"

"We're having a picnic! We were hitching through! We're just having the shittest picnic ever!"

I am pulling off my glasses and folding them to place into my pocket, staring readily at the security guard and his more nervous cohorts. They sense my fearlessness, my relentless swirling movement. I feel good, hearing my voice chattering in automatic, happy to have a human-sized target to address my rage to.

"You're assaulting me. You put your hands on me first. We are lost and came for a picnic. You started the violence. I'm taking my glasses off."

At any moment I am expecting a rabbit-punch to the face, for my arm to be twisted and locked into a pain-grip, for them to try to kick my legs out from under me and force me into the mud, any of the many and varied ways I have been brutalised and apprehended by authority over the last few years. Yet the fat security guard seems unsure of what to do now that he has grabbed my jacket, the others hesitant at seeing the situation escalating so quickly.

"George! Stop it!"

"No! He has to let go of me! He attacked me!"

I see the next slope, covered in thick brush, and whirl and tumble towards it, leaning backwards and letting myself drop into a freefall that breaks the security guard's grip but leaves me prone on my back. I am prostrate on my back tangled in the natural barbwire of bushy thorns. The first guard grabs my booted feet and pulls my legs apart, stamping quickly and suddenly between my legs three times in quick succession.

I brace, but there is no pain. Perhaps it is two days awake on amphetamine, or by some weird chance the angle I fell at means that his boot falls against my pubic bone instead of my junk, but he looks shocked and suddenly aware that my feet are easily at the height of his head, and to warn him I slow-motion swing a size 14 steel toecap boot past his nose, coiling another foot back in readiness to snap out to him.

My plan works, he has let me go and the other guards haven't followed, but I am now almost upside down on a slope in a bush staring up at a clear blue sky and watching events descend into farce. Most concerning is that I can't see what was happening to the others, just hearing them arguing with people responding in German.

The guard seems embarrassed: "Come on, get out of the bush."

"No. You assaulted me. Call the cops."

"The *polizei* are coming. Why are you here?"

"Good. I want them to. We were lost. We were having a picnic. We got lost. We were hitch-hiking."

"Mierda! Mierda? Are you OK?"

"Yeah, I'm ok."

"George! Shut up! Come up here."

"No I think I'm all right here. Naiad? Naiad? Are you OK?"

"Yeah I'm OK."

OK. We were all OK then.

"There aren't any signs up. How do we know it's private land? Can't RWE afford signs?"

One of them jumps delightedly at the mention.

"Ah, so you have heard of RWE then?"

The *polizei* arrive and hardly help the situation.

"Activisten? Activisten? Activisten?" One keeps repeating, pointing at us. Then he nods and smiles to the others. *"Activisten aus* London."

As the *polizei* arrive I climb out of the bushes and stand next to Mierda.

Mierda loses it, in a perfectly timed paddy, pulling items out of the cloth bag and throwing them on the hood of the car. It does look all quite innocuous.

"*Activisten*?" A notebook covered in scratchy ink illustrations.

"*Activisten*?" A little lunchbox full of pens with My Little Pony stickers on it.

"*Activisten*?" A bag of bananas.

I put my glasses back on.

It's true, we aren't any kind of activists. Just anarcho-tourists. Emphasis on the narco.

The main issue now seems to be that we have left all our ID back at the van, which is at the camp, and under no circumstances do we want to give the cops the excuse to search that van.

"We left the van in Cologne. Our IDs are there."

"You are staying at the camp."

"What camp?"

"The protest camp."

"What protest camp?"

This goes on for some time, but the three of us quickly pick up the story from each other that we hitch-hiked out of Cologne on some whim to follow someone's advice for a nice picnic spot. They manage to confirm Mierda and Naiad's IDs, probably because they were arrested in Berlin two years before shoplifting in Didl, but for me, it's the back of the van and a ride to the cells.

I am relieved that Naiad and Mierda are being released, and resign myself to the fate of the van. As I get in, I remove my glasses again, and brace myself for the polizei opposite to suddenly let fly with the fists, mentally preparing myself for blows to the face, stomach, chest in punishment.

Mierda shouts: "We'll get the ID and come after you."

"Ok, see you there."

The car pulls away. I wait expectantly for the cop opposite to lash out in his little latex gloves.

I ask after a little while.

"So, how far away is the station?"

"Ten minutes."

An hour later we arrive. I am led to the cell, removing jewellery, jacket, shoes at the door, and then put inside. Two cops watch from the doorway, eyes like a Hollywood mogul eying a new starlet on the casting couch.

I remove all my clothes, defiantly presenting my junk to them.

I am commanded to bend over.

I prepare myself for an internal search, legs spread, hands against the cell wall.

I smile. I have never felt more alive.

"Good times everybody, good times."

Roll credits.

Cable Street, Limehouse, June 2018.

Also by George F.

From Influx Press

Total Shambles

After slipping through the cracks of modern life and into the amoral underground beyond work-a-day society, George F finds himself at the heart of London's political frontline, where anarchy, alcohol and addiction stalk the streets of a different city than the one you know. From life on the street to behind the barricades, from the occupation of derelict buildings to inevitable evictions and confrontation with law and order, from euphoria to despair, *Total Shambles* follows the journey of an idealistic writer as he tries to thrive and survive in the contentious world of squatting in London.

Dodgy on the edge, or edgy on the dodge? Either way, George F's thunderous declamation against the enforced poverty of those who choose to exist on the other side of the lines, and possibly beyond the pale, acts as a salutary lesson in the florid hardships and plain hard work of "alternative lifestyles": you can make it if you can take it – few can.
Penny Rimbaud, *Crass*

A fantastic read for anyone interested in the underbelly of London.
The Guardian

Life behind the Sitex door...a series of confrontations from the contested margins of urban living, full of stories about how to live when there is (apparently) nowhere to live.
George McKay, author of Senseless Acts of Beauty and *DIY Culture*

Also by George F.

Total Shambles *is a fantastic piece of work, everything that writing should be – funny, moving, exciting, wild. A history lesson, a polemic, a picaresque adventure story, and, at big and pulsing heart, an attack on the shameless, state-encouraged worship of money and power and possessions and the tiny-mindedness and shrivelling of soul that is its consequence. Proof, if any more were needed, of the necessity of disobedience. It also contains the best description of a ketamine hit I've ever read.*
Niall Griffiths

I washed the taste of failure away with George F's rebarbative and in the end heart-breaking memoir of London squatting.
M John Harrison

Parts of "The Shittest Picnic Ever" first appeared in *Reckoning Magazine* (Issue #1) under the title *In Hambach Forst*.

A version of "From Paris, With Rage" first appeared in *Reckoning Magazine* (Issue #2).

Mother Black Cunt's Revenge first appeared in *An Unreliable Guide To London* and is reproduced here with permission of Influx Press.

All photos courtesy of 1slutriot. You can see more of Mierda's artwork at www.oneslutriot.com

zero books

CULTURE, SOCIETY & POLITICS

Contemporary culture has eliminated the concept and public figure of the intellectual. A cretinous anti-intellectualism presides, cheer-led by hacks in the pay of multinational corporations who reassure their bored readers that there is no need to rouse themselves from their stupor. Zer0 Books knows that another kind of discourse – intellectual without being academic, popular without being populist – is not only possible: it is already flourishing. Zer0 is convinced that in the unthinking, blandly consensual culture in which we live, critical and engaged theoretical reflection is more important than ever before.

If you have enjoyed this book, why not tell other readers by posting a review on your preferred book site.

Recent bestsellers from Zero Books are:

In the Dust of This Planet
Horror of Philosophy vol. 1
Eugene Thacker
In the first of a series of three books on the Horror of Philosophy, *In the Dust of This Planet* offers the genre of horror as a way of thinking about the unthinkable.
Paperback: 978-1-84694-676-9 ebook: 978-1-78099-010-1

Capitalist Realism
Is there no alternative?
Mark Fisher
An analysis of the ways in which capitalism has presented itself as the only realistic political-economic system.
Paperback: 978-1-84694-317-1 ebook: 978-1-78099-734-6

Rebel Rebel
Chris O'Leary
David Bowie: every single song. Everything you want to know, everything you didn't know.
Paperback: 978-1-78099-244-0 ebook: 978-1-78099-713-1

Cartographies of the Absolute
Alberto Toscano, Jeff Kinkle
An aesthetics of the economy for the twenty-first century.
Paperback: 978-1-78099-275-4 ebook: 978-1-78279-973-3

Romeo and Juliet in Palestine
Teaching Under Occupation
Tom Sperlinger
Life in the West Bank, the nature of pedagogy and the role of a university under occupation.
Paperback: 978-1-78279-637-4 ebook: 978-1-78279-636-7

Malign Velocities

Accelerationism and Capitalism

Benjamin Noys

Long listed for the Bread and Roses Prize 2015, *Malign Velocities* argues against the need for speed, tracking acceleration as the symptom of the ongoing crises of capitalism.

Paperback: 978-1-78279-300-7 ebook: 978-1-78279-299-4

Meat Market

Female Flesh under Capitalism

Laurie Penny

A feminist dissection of women's bodies as the fleshy fulcrum of capitalist cannibalism, whereby women are both consumers and consumed.

Paperback: 978-1-84694-521-2 ebook: 978-1-84694-782-7

Poor but Sexy

Culture Clashes in Europe East and West

Agata Pyzik

How the East stayed East and the West stayed West.

Paperback: 978-1-78099-394-2 ebook: 978-1-78099-395-9

Sweetening the Pill

or How We Got Hooked on Hormonal Birth Control

Holly Grigg-Spall

Has contraception liberated or oppressed women? *Sweetening the Pill* breaks the silence on the dark side of hormonal contraception.

Paperback: 978-1-78099-607-3 ebook: 978-1-78099-608-0

Why Are We The Good Guys?
Reclaiming your Mind from the Delusions of Propaganda
David Cromwell
A provocative challenge to the standard ideology that Western power is a benevolent force in the world.
Paperback: 978-1-78099-365-2 ebook: 978-1-78099-366-9